ANTI-SEMITISM ACROSS BORDERS

HEARING

BEFORE THE

SUBCOMMITTEE ON AFRICA, GLOBAL HEALTH, GLOBAL HUMAN RIGHTS, AND INTERNATIONAL ORGANIZATIONS

OF THE

COMMITTEE ON FOREIGN AFFAIRS
HOUSE OF REPRESENTATIVES

ONE HUNDRED FIFTEENTH CONGRESS

FIRST SESSION

MARCH 22, 2017

Serial No. 115–10

Printed for the use of the Committee on Foreign Affairs

Available via the World Wide Web: http://www.foreignaffairs.house.gov/ or http://www.gpo.gov/fdsys/

U.S. GOVERNMENT PUBLISHING OFFICE

24–753PDF   WASHINGTON : 2017

For sale by the Superintendent of Documents, U.S. Government Publishing Office
Internet: bookstore.gpo.gov   Phone: toll free (866) 512–1800; DC area (202) 512–1800
Fax: (202) 512–2104   Mail: Stop IDCC, Washington, DC 20402–0001

COMMITTEE ON FOREIGN AFFAIRS

EDWARD R. ROYCE, California, *Chairman*

CHRISTOPHER H. SMITH, New Jersey
ILEANA ROS-LEHTINEN, Florida
DANA ROHRABACHER, California
STEVE CHABOT, Ohio
JOE WILSON, South Carolina
MICHAEL T. McCAUL, Texas
TED POE, Texas
DARRELL E. ISSA, California
TOM MARINO, Pennsylvania
JEFF DUNCAN, South Carolina
MO BROOKS, Alabama
PAUL COOK, California
SCOTT PERRY, Pennsylvania
RON DeSANTIS, Florida
MARK MEADOWS, North Carolina
TED S. YOHO, Florida
ADAM KINZINGER, Illinois
LEE M. ZELDIN, New York
DANIEL M. DONOVAN, JR., New York
F. JAMES SENSENBRENNER, JR.,
  Wisconsin
ANN WAGNER, Missouri
BRIAN J. MAST, Florida
FRANCIS ROONEY, Florida
BRIAN K. FITZPATRICK, Pennsylvania
THOMAS A. GARRETT, JR., Virginia

ELIOT L. ENGEL, New York
BRAD SHERMAN, California
GREGORY W. MEEKS, New York
ALBIO SIRES, New Jersey
GERALD E. CONNOLLY, Virginia
THEODORE E. DEUTCH, Florida
KAREN BASS, California
WILLIAM R. KEATING, Massachusetts
DAVID N. CICILLINE, Rhode Island
AMI BERA, California
LOIS FRANKEL, Florida
TULSI GABBARD, Hawaii
JOAQUIN CASTRO, Texas
ROBIN L. KELLY, Illinois
BRENDAN F. BOYLE, Pennsylvania
DINA TITUS, Nevada
NORMA J. TORRES, California
BRADLEY SCOTT SCHNEIDER, Illinois
THOMAS R. SUOZZI, New York
ADRIANO ESPAILLAT, New York
TED LIEU, California

AMY PORTER, *Chief of Staff*   THOMAS SHEEHY, *Staff Director*
JASON STEINBAUM, *Democratic Staff Director*

———

SUBCOMMITTEE ON AFRICA, GLOBAL HEALTH, GLOBAL HUMAN RIGHTS, AND INTERNATIONAL ORGANIZATIONS

CHRISTOPHER H. SMITH, New Jersey, *Chairman*

MARK MEADOWS, North Carolina
DANIEL M. DONOVAN, JR., New York
F. JAMES SENSENBRENNER, JR.,
  Wisconsin
THOMAS A. GARRETT, JR., Virginia

KAREN BASS, California
AMI BERA, California
JOAQUIN CASTRO, Texas
THOMAS R. SUOZZI, New York

CONTENTS

Page

WITNESSES

Mr. Paul Goldenberg, national director, Secure Community Network 7
Ms. Stacy Burdett, vice president, Government Relations, Advocacy, and Community Engagement, Anti-Defamation League 15
    Rabbi Andrew Baker, personal representative on combating anti-Semitism, Office of the Chairperson-in-Office, Organization for Security and Co-operation in Europe 26
    Mr. Mark Weitzman, director of government affairs, Simon Wiesenthal Center 35

LETTERS, STATEMENTS, ETC., SUBMITTED FOR THE HEARING

Mr. Paul Goldenberg: Prepared statement 11
Ms. Stacy Burdett: Prepared statement 18
Rabbi Andrew Baker: Prepared statement 30
Mr. Mark Weitzman: Prepared statement 39

APPENDIX

Hearing notice 70
Hearing minutes 71
Ms. Stacy Burdett:
    List of cities with no reports of hate crimes 72
    ADL and HRF Scorecard on Hate Crime Response in the OSCE Region 74
    The Honorable Christopher H. Smith, a Representative in Congress from the State of New Jersey, and chairman, Subcommittee on Africa, Global Health, Global Human Rights, and International Organizations:
Wisenthal Center's Overview of Digital Terrorism and Hate 76
State Department definition and examples of anti-Semitism 78
Statement of the Union of Orthodox Jewish Congregations of America 79
Statement of B'nai B'rith International 80

ANTI-SEMITISM ACROSS BORDERS

WEDNESDAY, MARCH 22, 2017

House of Representatives,
Subcommittee on Africa, Global Health,
Global Human Rights, and International Organizations,
Committee on Foreign Affairs,
Washington, DC.

The subcommittee met, pursuant to notice, at 10:02 a.m., in room 2172, Rayburn House Office Building, Hon. Christopher H. Smith (chairman of the subcommittee) presiding.

Mr. SMITH. The subcommittee will come to order. And good morning and welcome, everyone. And I thank you for being here for this very, very timely and, I think, very important hearing.

The Jewish people have survived and thrived from the times of biblical antiquity to the present day—quite a feat when you consider all of the civilizations that have come and gone: The Hittites, the Assyrians, the Egyptians, Persians, Greece, and Rome. The presence of Jews has enriched the cultures of many civilizations and countries, from the Americas, to Ethiopia, to China.

But just as the Jewish people have endured, so too, has anti-Semite hatred. This hatred has ranged from prejudiced slurs whispered in private to the murder of more than 6 million Jews in the Holocaust.

Seventy-two years after the Holocaust ended, anti-Semites continue to target the Jewish people for discrimination, destruction of property, and even death. This hearing will explore global threats to Jewish communities, the underlying ideologies, and what actions the United States and other countries and international organizations should take.

Our witnesses, including Paul Goldenberg, the national director of the Secure Community Network, addresses "the current state of affairs in Europe, specifically the increased levels of hate-motivated incidents impacting Jewish communities." Mr. Goldenberg also asks whether perpetrators on both sides of the Atlantic may be feeding each other.

He emphasizes that it is vital that the Congress and the U.S. Government identify, analyze, and respond to the cross-Atlantic links between anti-Semitism and anti-Semitic remarks. I convened this hearing so that we can ensure that we are scrutinizing the cross-Atlantic connections and the solutions.

Our second witness, Rabbi Andy Baker, a friend for decades and personal representative of the OSCE co-chair-in-office on combating anti-Semitism and director of international Jewish affairs for the

American Jewish Committee, testifies in his written remarks that, after the terrorist attacks in Paris, Brussels, and Copenhagen,"no longer were governments able to ignore the situation. They have responded."

He cautioned, though, that "problems still remain. Governments have taken different approaches, and some only in stop-gap measures." Rabbi Baker has warned that we need to be clear-eyed in confronting and combating anti-Semitism, which manifests itself on both the right and the left.

And I would note parenthetically, as the one who suggested we have an OSCE conference back in the year 2000—and, thankfully, Ambassador Minikes, who was our OSCE Ambassador at the time, made that dream, working with Andy Baker and a few other leaders, a reality during the Bush administration. Andy was the one who wordsmithed the language that became, major parts of it, what we call the Berlin Declaration, which was an action plan for the countries of the OSCE—Canada, the United States, and Europe, Eastern Europe, and Russia—to combat this pervasive violence against Jews called anti-Semitism.

It was a very important and, I think, remarkable document. It is still in force, although its implementation—and that is one of the things that Rabbi Baker seeks to do as Special Representative, to talk to countries, their governments, to the NGOs in country to try to persuade them to be far more proactive than so many of them are.

In his written testimony, our third witness, Mark Weitzman, director of government affairs for the Simon Wiesenthal Center, explored a wide range of ideologies and manifestations of anti-Semitism. He flagged that the "regeneration of traditional anti-Semitism is all the more dangerous because, unlike the violent extremists of both left and right in radical Islam, it is now found in government circles and halls of power in countries that we define as Western democracies."

Pointing to a trend in Europe and the United States, Mr. Weitzman notes that "academic spaces are quickly becoming hotbeds of anti-Jewish bias, with students each year reporting greater discomfort at publicly identifying as Jewish or as supporters of Israel."

The great Natan Sharansky has taught us powerfully about the "new anti-Semitism" which targets the State of Israel. I will never forget when Natan Sharansky testified at two hearings that I chaired. This is about the 18th or 19th hearing on combating anti-Semitism. He talked about demonization, delegitimization, and the double standard—the three D's, as he called it—of modern-day anti-Semitism, on top of, of course, the virulent form that we have known for millennia of targeting Jews, killing Jews, and destroying Jewish cemeteries, and all of the rest of the hate manifestations. But Sharansky made an excellent point, and he made it at the Berlin Conference—and Rabbi Baker, I am sure, remembers it well—when he told all of the foreign ministers and everybody who was assembled about the three D's. He said, disagree with Israel on a policy, but as soon as you cross that line and the double stand- ard and say they don't have a right to exist or they get dispropor- tionate focus at the U.N. Human Rights Council and a number of other U.N. agencies—when you demonize Israel, as they do so frequently, where is China? Talk about human rights abuse. There is the human rights abuser of the world, not Israel, and yet Israel gets all the attention. And then, of course, this idea of a double standard, which is rampant.

It is a virus, anti-Semitism, that, again, causes the U.N. Human Rights Council to make Israel the only country permanently on its debate agenda—the only country.

In this context, I applaud our new Permanent Representative to the U.N., Ambassador Nikki Haley—and I have met with Nikki Haley on this very issue—for announcing on Monday that the U.S. will no longer participate in this frenzy of Israel-bashing known as "Agenda Item 7." Instead, she said, the United States will only participate "to vote against the outrageous, one-sided, anti-Israel resolutions that so diminish what the Human Rights Council should be."

The Human Rights Council is also the body that directed the High Commissioner for Human Rights to compile a blacklist of companies working with Israelis beyond the 1949 armistice line, including Jerusalem's Old City, the location of Judaism's holiest site. This measure is self-evidently born out of the anti-Israeli boycott, divestment, and sanctions, or BDS, movement that is disturbingly present in many European countries and on college campuses across the United States.

I have met with the High Commissioner for Human Rights and raised this issue myself last fall and said how disappointed, how angry so many of us are that he would misuse his position as High Commissioner to carry on in this way. And, of course, the Human Rights Council is doing it on steroids.

Let me also say, before I introduce our witness, I want to also welcome Stacy Burdett from the ADL, again, another longtime friend and a great leader in combating anti-Semitism. She has also brought a particular focus to Latin America, a much welcomed focus.

But for all of your wonderful work, thank you, as well for your leadership.

Finally, I would also like to associate myself with Mr. Weitzman's statement when he put it, "Fighting anti-Semitism always has been a bipartisan commitment, and in today's fractured political world it is more necessary than ever that the U.S. maintain its diplomatic and moral leadership in this issue."

And I really thank you for that admonishment, which is so important. This has to stay bipartisan, because we as Americans have to combat anti-Semitism anytime and anywhere it manifests its ugly face. For as long as I have been a Member of Congress, there has been broad bipartisan support for combating anti-Semitism.

Just for the record, in 1982, on my first trip, David Harris now with the AJC, and a number of other important leaders, Mark Levin from the National Conference on Soviet Jewry, invited me to go to Moscow and Leningrad for 10 days to meet with refuseniks. And what an eye-opening experience it was to see when there is a state sponsor of anti-Semitism—that is, the Soviet Union—and the systematic persecution of Jews in psychiatric prisons and, of course, by making anyone who applied for an exit visa poor by denying them a job, not giving an exit visa and then making them poor by denying them any means to provide for their families. And then, of course, prison was commonplace.

I visited Perm Camp 35 in the Ural Mountains a few years later, as a matter of fact, along with Frank Wolf. We went and videotaped every prisoner we met with. It was at the beginnings of glasnost and perestroika. And when we showed that to Natan Sharansky, who had just been released, he said, these were all of my friends, and they are still there. And, of course, we kept fighting until they got out.

This hearing will be the first in a series that our subcommittee will conduct. Our next hearing, we hope to have the Special Envoy, when he or she is named—and it may be somebody sitting at this very witness table—to be the Special Envoy to Monitor and Combat Anti-Semitism.

For the record, back in 2004, I am the one who offered the amendment to create it. It is a statutory position, and I, along with the other co-chairs of the Anti-Semitism Caucus, have done a joint letter asking that the administration name that person now. And earlier this week, in a meeting with Vice President Pence, not only did I raise this issue but gave him a letter asking that that person be named now, because there is so much to do with by that individual and for that office.

I would like to yield now to the ranking member, Ms. Bass, for any opening comments she would have.

Ms. Bass. Thank you very much, Mr. Chair. As I listen to your comments, one more time I will tell you that I think you need to do a book talking about your three-decade experience in fighting for human rights. And I think your opening statement was another example of that.

I want to welcome the witness and the members of the audience. Thank you for being here.

We are here this morning to hear from our expert witness about what is growing anti-Semitism across borders. What is most important to me is not to hear only the perspective of the witnesses on the reasons for increased incidents of anti-Semitism in the world but to learn where this trend is most prevalent overseas and who is behind the rise in anti-Semitism.

Equally important is to learn how these trends must be dealt with, assertively or otherwise. I believe that these trends must be dealt with assertively and that the United States must take a leadership role in such efforts. We can't look the other way, either overseas or domestically, regarding anti-Semitism. We must stand up against all forms of bias. We can't pick and choose when it is convenient to stand against bias and when it is not. We must call it out wherever we see it.

The role of the Special Envoy to Monitor and Combat Anti-Semitism came into being by way of the Global Anti-Semitism Review Act of 2004 that the chairman spoke about—because he authored it. I also believe that it is critical to have a special envoy at the State Department responsible for addressing anti-Semitism globally. I oppose reported attempts by the administration to cut funding for the Special Envoy. I think it is a position with the goal of monitoring and combating anti-Semitism worldwide, and the reestablishment of this position is a priority.

I also want to say that, while today's hearing is to address what is going on around the world, we do need to acknowledge what is going on in our own country. We need to acknowledge the fact that there have been threats at Jewish community centers around the country, there has been desecration of Jewish cemeteries.

The community that I represent in Los Angeles, a large part of it is the Jewish community, and there have been numerous threats to the Jewish community centers in my district. In fact, I am meeting with a group of constituents from one of those centers in the next couple of weeks when we are on our break.

I yield back.

Mr. SMITH. Thank you, Ms. Bass. And I appreciate your very kind comments. And I reciprocate and thank you for your leadership for all these years too, both in the State legislature and now here in Washington.

And you are right; the immediate genesis for this hearing was what is happening in the United States. We are the Foreign Affairs Committee, but the linkages, obviously, between the two are inescapable. So thank you for underscoring that so well.

Mr. Suozzi.

Mr. SUOZZI. I want to thank you also, Mr. Chairman. This is the first time I heard you speak at length on this, as a freshman, and I am very impressed by all the things that you have done throughout your career and the things that you had to say today. And I am looking forward to working in a bipartisan fashion to combat this evil in the world.

This is very important in my district, and people in my district are very concerned about this issue. We have had many threats at our Jewish community centers, and we read the reports of what is going on throughout the world.

So I want to thank you for your leadership, and I want to thank the ranking member for her leadership as well.

Mr. SMITH. Thank you, Mr. Suozzi.

Mr. Schneider.

Mr. SCHNEIDER. Thank you.

And I will echo and associate myself with the words complimenting the chairman for all of his work and commitment to this issue.

In my district, this is an issue that is affecting many of the institutions. Anti-Semitism is affecting institutions in Chicago, throughout the country. It is something of grave concern. As a Jewish Member of Congress, this is an issue that is also very personal.

And while I don't have prepared remarks, I would like to share a very brief story. I got a letter from my cousin when I first came to Congress 4 years ago reminding me that his grandfather, my great-uncle, my grandmother's brother, used to keep a chocolate bar in his drawer. And he did it as a reminder of what this country offered.

My grandmother's family came from Kiev. They fled the pogroms in 1912. And that chocolate bar was a reminder of the opportunity of this great country but also a reminder to him of where they came from and that they needed to be prepared to move at any moment, because, as Jews, they were always under threat.

And at that time, when I received the letter from my cousin Jordan, I thought, yes, but we are in a different place now. Four years later, we are seeing a rise of anti-Semitism around the globe and in this country.

Jordan wrote me a letter recently, talking about his family on the other side, because the family we share has grown. They came here in 1912. There are over 100 in the next generation, in my generation and our children's generation. But on Jordan's other side, that family was in Gorno. They were not able to come into this country. They were denied access. And they were completely wiped out in the Holocaust.

They understand, my family understands the impact of anti-Semitism and what it can do. And we need to be prepared to address it.

In January 2015, I went to France with Jewish Federations of North America to talk to the community there shortly after the Charlie Hebdo and Hypercacher attacks. France, as you will touch on in your testimony, has taken direct steps to address anti-Semitism in its country, and we have seen good progress. We need to continue to do that in this country. We need to work with our allies around the world and stand up wherever we can.

So this is a very important hearing. Thank you, Mr. Chairman, for taking the lead in calling this hearing.

I want to thank the witnesses for your testimony, but, more importantly, thank you for the work you and your institutions do in standing up to anti-Semitism here and around the world.

We need to make sure that "Never again" is not just a motto but is a reality and that we address anti-Semitism, because it doesn't just affect Jews, it affects everybody.

Thank you very much. And I yield back.

Mr. SMITH. Mr. Schneider, thank you very much for your very strong comments.

I would like to now introduce our distinguished witnesses, beginning first with Mr. Paul Goldenberg, who is the national director of the Secure Community Network. He is also chairman and president of Cardinal Point Strategies and a member of the U.S. Department of Homeland Security's Advisory Council. He is the former vice chair of the U.S. Department of Homeland Security's Faith-Based Council and is senior adviser to the Department's newly established Countering Violent Extremism initiative.

Mr. Goldenberg is a senior adviser to the Faith-Based Community Security Program at Rutgers University and, in that capacity, has worked closely on the ground with European Jewish communities and European Jewish security groups and, I would note parenthetically, years back, was the chief promoter and architect of an initiative to train the trainers, which had a very, very laudable impact on law enforcement and recognizing anti-Semitism for what it was and not being just disregarded as hooliganism or some other crime, looking at that motive. And he was very, very instrumental in that.

I would like to then introduce our second witness, Rabbi Andy Baker, who is director of international Jewish affairs for the American Jewish Community and the personal representative of the Organization for Security and Cooperation in Europe's chair-in-office on combating anti-Semitism. He is responsible for maintaining and developing AJC's network of relationships with Jewish communities throughout the diaspora and addressing the accompanying international issues and concerns.

He has been a prominent leader in addressing Holocaust-era issues in Europe and in international efforts to combat anti-Semitism. Rabbi Baker has served as the president of the Washington Board of Rabbis, president of the Interfaith Conference of Washington, and commissioner on the District of Columbia's Human Rights Commission.

We will then hear from Mark Weitzman, who is director of government affairs and the director of the Task Force Against Hate and Terrorism for the Wiesenthal Center. He is also the chief representative of the Center to the United Nations in New York.

Mr. Weitzman is a member of the official U.S. delegation to the International Holocaust Remembrance Alliance, where he chairs the Committee on Anti-Semitism and Holocaust Denial. He also co-chairs the Working Group on International Affairs of the Global Forum on Anti-Semitism. Mr. Weitzman has authored many publications and books and is the winner of the 2007 National Jewish Book Award for best anthology for anti-Semitism.

We will then hear from Ms. Stacy Burdett, who is the Anti-Defamation League's vice president for government relations, advocacy, and community engagement. She heads the Government and National Affairs Office, which represents ADL to the Federal Government, foreign Embassies, and policy community on a full range of ADL issues.

As lead lobbyist on international issues, Ms. Burdett is the face of ADL to Congress, the administration, and foreign diplomats. And, as I said a moment ago, I have known Stacy for so many years and so deeply appreciate her great leadership in this great and important fight.

I would like to now yield to Mr. Goldenberg for his opening.

STATEMENT OF MR. PAUL GOLDENBERG, NATIONAL DIRECTOR, SECURE COMMUNITY NETWORK

Mr. GOLDENBERG. Thank you. And it is an honor and privilege for me to be here today. I apologize for being a bit tardy. I think I rang off too many bells at the security checkpoint outside, which is not the first time.

So, Mr. Chairman, thank you again for allowing me to testify today regarding the current state of affairs in Europe, specifically the increased levels of hate-motivated incidents impacting Jewish communities. There has also been a wave, as we all know in this room, of similar events here in the United States, where perpetrators on both sides of the Atlantic unfortunately may be feeding into each other.

I am both proud and honored to be here with such a distinguished group of colleagues today. And I applaud you and your subcommittee for the steadfast commitment and unwavering support.

In 2004, as you know, Congressman Smith appointed me to work overseas through the good efforts of the OSCE, so I speak to you today through a different set of optics. I am a former law enforcement veteran, and, as they say in the business, I see things quite differently. We worked across 10 European nations, working hand-in-hand with Andy Baker, Mark, and our colleagues at the Anti-Defamation League for nearly 7 years.

Over the past 2 years, I have had the privilege of working closely with the Faith-Based Security Program at Rutgers University, where we are now working abroad in places like Molenbeek, Brussels, and Copenhagen. And as part of this new initiative under the leadership of former Attorney General John Farmer, we have made countless trips in recent months abroad traveling to multiple European cities. So we speak with some passion on this subject.

Through these trips, I have been able to gain a firsthand understanding of the current climate, hearing the concerns of Jewish communities under threat and assessing what we can all do collaboratively to assist them.

Just 2 weeks ago, I sat with the Chief Rabbi of Belgium in the Great Synagogue in Brussels, an institution that survived several wars, still stood strong after the Holocaust—a beautiful, celebrated structure that once again is surrounded by armed paratroop soldiers with long assault rifles. However, they serve not as an occupying or threatening force but as protectors of a community.

And similar scenes, we all know, are in Belgium, France, Denmark, and other Western nations—armed military troops once again surrounding Jewish institutions just decades after the Holocaust.

Consider the United Kingdom. There were a record number of anti-Semitic offenses in 2016. The Community Security Trust recorded 1,309 anti-Semitic incidents nationwide during that year, a 36-percent increase from the 960 recorded by the CST in 2015.

Previously, record-high occurrences have been triggered by anti-Semitic reactions to sudden, specific geopolitical events, leading to temporary spikes in occurrences. In contrast—and I can say almost the same for here in the United States—there was no single, sudden event in 2016.

In 2014, for instance, there were 1,182 incidents recorded up until that year. This previous highest total coincided with a conflict between Israel and Hamas, which saw a global, again, rise in anti-Semitism and incidents of a similar nature. In contrast, as I stated, there was no single, sudden trigger event in 2016. And these high numbers of incidents both here and abroad, I have used the term, are unprecedented.

In Germany, according to the Coordination Forum for Countering Anti-Semitism, the CFCA, anti-Semitism has increased in parallel, as they note, "to the general rise of far-right crime since the beginning of the migrant crisis." The number of criminal investigations opened following attacks on Jews, Jewish property, and hate speech against Jews amounted to 2,083 cases during 2015, an increase of 201 percent from the previous year.

And as I heard Mr. Schneider, Congressman Schneider, a glimmer of hope still exists in France. Following years of significant incidents and attacks, the same CFCA report notes a significant de-

cline of anti-Semitic incidents in 2016, after 2015 was characterized by a rise of anti-Semitic incidents.

Experts that I have spoken to, and many of us have collaborated
with, attribute the decline to a strong and swift response by the
government in launching a campaign against anti-Semitism in the
country. First and foremost, that means engaging with the nation's
law enforcement forces and agencies.

As a result, Jewish communities abroad are not only rethinking
their approach to security, they are already changing their daily
routines, adopting new ways of doing things, and deciding when
and where to go—from synagogue to grocery store—based not on
their desires, but on their fears and insecurity.

I had the privilege to testify last April before the Commission on
Security and Cooperation in Europe on anticipating and preventing
deadly attacks on European Jewish communities. The concerns expressed then and the premonitions made regarding the migration
of hatred, particularly anti-Semitism, has unfortunately manifested
itself in the form of bomb threats, hate crimes, and cemetery desecrations, as we have seen as of late right here in the United States.
Evermore connected, these extremist groups in the United States
are borrowing, adapting, and enhancing the tactics and strategies
adapted and adopted in Europe.

Just a few more statistics, unfortunately. According to a recently
distributed report by the New York City Police Department, they
found that hate crimes against Jewish people more than doubled
in the city since the start of the new year as compared to the same
time period in 2016. The report documents 56 hate crimes from
January 1 to February 12, with 28 incidents targeting Jews. In the
same 6-week period the previous year, the total number of hate
crimes recorded in New York City was only 31, with 13 targeting
Jews.

A recent ADL report on anti-Semitic acts that targeted journalists between August 2015 and July 2016 uncovered an   astonishing
2.6 million tweets containing language frequently used in anti-Semitic speech—again, an unprecedented number.

As part of our own independent research, with regard to statistics, just over the last 75 days in the United States of America, from
January 1 to March 13, 307—and that number is fluid, it is
changing—307 anti-Jewish incidents across 40 States in 75 days.
Since the beginning of the year, we have exceeded 170 bomb threats
phoned in or emailed to 117 Jewish institutions, centers, schools,
ADL offices, and other establishments, leading to massive
disruptions and evacuations of thousands of people, to include   children and infants.

Indeed, one of the most enduring images of 2017 for the Jewish
community may be the scenes of children being rushed into the
freezing winter temperatures to evacuate JCCs right in our own
backyards, and those of empty cribs abandoned in parking lots, as
dedicated staff members, infants, and toddlers rolled these mecha-
nisms out of their facilities to safe locations.

This phenomenon can be summed up briefly by sharing one incident in Whitefish that we need to note for the record. Whitefish,
Montana—a small, pristine, beautiful town with warm and welcoming people. The location hosts, in addition to a small commu-

nity, one of the most well-known members of the white supremacist movement in the country.

As Jews throughout the United States were readying their homes for Hanukkah celebration, the Jewish community of Whitefish was courageously dealing with intimidation, threats of violence, and harassment from outside agitators. Marches, armed marches, were threatened against Jews. Fake news stories alleging conspiracies by the Jewish community of Whitefish against their longtime neighbors were alleged. And here is the most egregious: The pictures of children of the rabbi and Jewish leaders were posted on neo-Nazi Web sites calling for the followers to troll and harass the children. Attacks that specifically target children are abhorrent and unthinkable and would have the capability to paralyze any American town anywhere in the United States.

In closing, beyond death and destruction, we know that these hate groups and terrorists, whether neo-Nazi, white supremacists, or Islamic extremists, they seek to create a sense of fear and vulnerability. If they are successful, this can be more impactful than any attack on us, the Jewish people, the American people, forcing us to not only query the safety and security of the societies we live in, but causing us to question our own ability to protect our neighborhoods and families and, with this, potentially causing us to change our behavior, retracting from our daily lives, our way of living, compromising our beliefs, whether that means altering how we dress or, even more disconcerting, after the recent bomb threats, hearing that some who have come to relish and rely on the remarkable services offered by these Jewish community centers—they will be reassessing their members, grounded on fear.

The American Jewish community very much remains open for business. We are back in our houses, we are back in our centers, we have been back in our schools, we are back in our institutions. We are training; we are working with our police agencies. The U.S. Department of Homeland Security and the FBI have done a remarkable job working with the community each and every day. So we are very much open for business, remain open.

I look forward to any questions that you may have, sir.

[The prepared statement of Mr. Goldenberg follows:]

Written Testimony for the Record

Testimony of Paul Goldenberg

National Director, Secure Community Network
Senior Advisor, Rutgers University Faith-Based Communities Security Program
Member, DHS Homeland Security Advisory Council

United States House of Representatives
Committee on Foreign Affairs
Subcommittee on Africa, Global Health, Global Human Rights, and International Organizations

"Anti-Semitism Across Borders"
Wednesday, March 22, 2017
10:00 AM
Rayburn House Office Building
Room 2172

Good Morning, Ladies and Gentlemen. My name is Paul Goldenberg. I currently serve as a senior advisor to the United States Department of Homeland Security as a member of the Secretary's Homeland Security Advisory Council (HSAC). In that capacity, I served on the Countering Violent Extremism Sub-Committee, Co-Chair the Foreign Fighter Task Force and am former Vice-Chair of the Faith-Based Advisory & Communications Sub-Committee. For the past decade, I now proudly serve as the National Director of the Secure Community Network (SCN), led by Michael Siegal, the official national homeland security initiative of the American Jewish community, working under the auspices of The Jewish Federations of North America and the Conference of Presidents of Major American Jewish Organizations.

Mr. Chairman: thank you for the opportunity to testify today about the current state of affairs in Europe, specifically the increased levels of hate motivated incidents impacting Jewish communities. There has also been a wave of such incidents here in the U.S. and perpetrators on both sides of the Atlantic may be feeding each other.

Over the past two years, I have had the privilege of working closely with the Faith-Based Communities Security Program at Rutgers University, a leading edge initiative that seeks to protect and secure vulnerable populations in Europe, an effort generously funded by Rutgers Law Alumnus Paul Miller. As a part of this new initiative, and working under the leadership of former New Jersey Attorney General John Farmer, we have made countless trips in recent months overseas, traveling to multiple European cities. Since its inception, the program has conducted threat assessments throughout Europe, in France, the UK, Sweden, Denmark, Czech Republic, Belgium among others, as well as key cities across the United States, with the ultimate goal of producing operational recommendations to combat extremist violence against religious, minority and other vulnerable communities, and providing the literature and training to implement such best practices.

Through these trips, I have been able to gain a first-hand understanding of the current climate, hearing the concerns of Jewish communities who are under threat, and assessing what we can do to best assist them. Just two weeks ago I sat with the Chief Rabbi of Belgium in the Great Synagogue of Brussels, an institution that survived several wars and still stood strong after the Holocaust. A beautiful and celebrated structure that once again is surrounded by soldiers with assault rifles, this time; however, they serve not as an occupying and or threating force, but as protectors of the community. Similar scenes are frequent in France, Denmark and other western nations.

Consider, the United Kingdom, there was a record number of anti-Semitic offenses recorded in 2016. The Community Security trust recorded 1,309 anti-Semitic incidents nationwide during that year, a 36% increase from the 960 recorded by CST in 2015. Previously, record high occurrences have been triggered by anti-Semitic reactions to sudden, specific 'geopolitical events' leading to temporary 'spikes' in occurrences. In contrast, there was no single, sudden trigger event in 2016. In 2014, for instance, there were 1,182 incidents recorded. Up until this year, this previous highest total coincided with a conflict between Israel and Hamas, which saw a global rise in anti-Semitic incidents. In contrast, however, there was no single, sudden trigger event in 2016, and the high number of incidents was spread uniformly through most of the year.

In Germany, according to the Coordination Forum for Countering Antisemitism (CFCA), anti-Semitism in Germany has increased in parallel to –as they note- the "general rise of far-right crime since the beginning of the migrant crisis." The number of criminal investigations opened following attacks on Jews, Jewish property and hate speech against Jews amounted to 2,083 cases during 2015, an increase of 201% from the previous year.

A glimmer of hope seems to exist in France, following years of significant incidents and attacks, the same CFCA report notes a "significant decline of anti-Semitic incidents in 2016 after 2015 has been characterized by a rise in anti-Semitic incidents." Experts attribute the decline to a strong and swift response by the government in launching a campaign against anti-Semitism across the country.

As a result of this, Jewish communities abroad are not only rethinking their approach to security, they are already changing their daily routines, adopting new ways of doing things, and deciding when and where to go – from Synagogue to the grocery store – based not on their desires, but on their fears and insecurities.

Ever-more connected, extremist groups in the United States are borrowing, adapting and enhancing the tactics and strategies adopted in Europe. Although not every anti-Semitic individual, group, manifestation, threat, or incident in Europe and the USA is connected, they are increasingly the context for each other. It is vital that the Congress, and U.S. government, identify, analyze, and respond to the cross-Atlantic links between anti-Semitism and anti-Semitic attacks.

Although the focus of this hearing is foreign countries, it is important to summarize what is happening in our country, so that you have a sense for how Jewish communities in the USA are now experiencing what Jewish communities in Europe have been undergoing and to inform your long-term examination of the cross-Atlantic connections.

While reliable, real-time data on hate crimes is often difficult to discern, the incoming data in recent months is troubling. The Southern Poverty Law Center recorded 1,094 bias-related harassment and intimidation incidents nationally since November 2016. According to a recently distributed report by the New York City Police Department, they found that hate crimes against Jewish people more than doubled in New York City since the start of the New Year, as compared

Written Testimony for the Record

to the same period in 2016; the report documents 56 hate crimes from January 1st to February 12th, with 28 incidents targeting Jews. In the same six week period the previous year, the total number of hate crimes recorded in New York City was only 31, with 13 targeting Jews. An ADL report on anti-Semitic acts that targeted journalists between August 2015 and July 2016 uncovered an astonishing 2.6 million tweets containing language frequently found in anti-Semitic speech. These tweets had an estimated 10 billion impressions (reach), likely contributing to the reinforcement and normalization of anti-Semitic language on a massive scale.

As part of our own independent research regarding the increase of anti-Jewish hate incidents, the Secure Community Network (SCN) includes open source reported statistics from January 1, 2017 through March 13, 2017. SCN's research recorded a record breaking 307 anti-Jewish incidents across forty (40) states in 75 days.

Since the beginning of the year, over 166 bomb threats were phoned in or emailed to 117 institutions, Jewish Community Centers, Schools, ADL offices and other Jewish establishments, leading to massive disruptions and the evacuation of thousands of people, to include children and infants. Indeed, one of the most enduring images of 2017 for the Jewish community may be the scenes of children being rushed into the freezing winter temperatures to evacuate JCCs, and those of empty cribs abandoned in parking lots, as dedicated staff members took infants and toddlers out of the facilities and sought safe locations for them.

This phenomenon can be summed up briefly by sharing one incident in Whitefish, Montana. A pristine, beautiful town filled with warm and welcoming people, this location hosts – in addition to a small but vibrant Jewish community –one of the most well-known members of the white supremacist movement in the country.

As Jews throughout the United States were readying their homes for Hanukah celebrations, the Jewish community of Whitefish was courageously dealing with intimidation, threats of violence and harassment from outside agitators. Marches against Jews were threatened, fake news stories alleging conspiracies by the Jewish community of Whitefish against their long-time neighbors were alleged, and the pictures of the children of Jewish community leaders were posted on neo-Nazi websites calling for followers to troll and harass the children. Attacks that specifically target children are abhorrent and unthinkable and would have the capability to paralyze any community's ability to function and thrive. The individuals behind these cowardly events – and those like them – know that if their actions can cause us to change our own routines, policies, positions or way of life, they can change the agenda and hold power, not just over political processes, but over our psychological ones as well.

Beyond death and destruction, hate groups and terrorists – whether neo-Nazis, white supremacists or Islamist extremists – seek to create a sense of fear and vulnerability. If they are successful, this can be more impactful than any attack, forcing us to not only query the safety and security of the societies that we live in, but causing us to question our own ability to protect our neighborhoods and families, and with this, causing us to change our behavior – retracting from our daily routines, way of living and compromising our beliefs – whether that means altering how we dress or pray, and even more disconcerting, after the recent bomb threats, hearing that some whom have come to relish and rely on the remarkable services offered by Jewish Community Centers, may be reassessing their memberships grounded on fear.

Written Testimony for the Record

We cannot voluntarily allow for what the terrorist organizations themselves could never have achieved on their own – by giving up our principles or way of life. A community immunized against the psychological influence of terrorist threats has a greater ability to resist manipulation. If those who undertake attacks or threaten our communities believe that they will not be able to create terror or panic, and a subsequent unraveling of our principles as a community, it eliminates a major cause for their activity. In this, through our own psychological strength and position, we may better mitigate against such threats or attacks and prevent them from disrupting our way of life.

The question of whether or not the American Jewish community is targeted by hatred and terror is not up for debate. Jews here and abroad remain targets. Tripwires around the world can trigger an attack; global conflict serves to put the entire Jewish community on alert. In this country, both law enforcement and the Jewish community recognize this unique reality and are taking proactive and exceptional measures to create a culture of security that joins the efforts of law enforcement – from local police departments to the FBI and Department of Homeland Security (DHS) – with the concerns of the Jewish community. We had recently met with Director Comey of the FBI and I can assure you that community leaders left this meeting with a high level of confidence and know that FBI, state, and local law enforcement support our efforts. The US Department of Homeland Security just deployed highly trained DHS professionals to Jewish Community Centers whom are providing training and additional resources.

By educating lay leaders, community members, staff and administrators as well as teachers, and by more effectively working with police, we have the fundamentals to empower ourselves, developing a sense of ownership among our whole community. Working with state and local authorities communities will better understand the resources and capabilities that government can provide during an incident, as well as what we need to do for our own communities thereafter.

Moving the Jewish community and all faith based communities beyond "awareness" to "engaged citizenry" must be a primary goal for 2017. We are and remain resilient…no other community understands better that life has its challenges and hardships; resiliency means that when confronted with such actions, we as a community will work to make them ultimately surmountable. Our community centers have become an oasis for all citizens. The organizations and people that administer these facilities understand the magnitude of security and safety.

After months of enduring 166 bomb threats across over forty (40) states, JCC members, parents and other guests have moved from fear and anxiety to defiant resolve and resilience. They refused to be driven from their schools and community spaces by cowardly acts of intolerance and hatred. In this, the hate and fear that seeks to divide us, has indeed united us even more so.
Thank you Mr. Chairman for the opportunity to testify in front of this Subcommittee today. I'm happy to address any question you or other Members may have.

Mr. SMITH. Mr. Goldenberg, thank you very much for that very, very powerful testimony and those insights.

Before going to our next witness, at the request of our distinguished ranking member, we will go to Stacy Burdett. She has invited her, and, unfortunately, the gentlelady has a schedule conflict that she has to be at. Ileana Ros-Lehtinen, same thing. She probably will come back.

But I would just note for the record that the chairman emeritus is the chairman of the Middle East and North Africa Subcommittee. She is a co-chair of the Bipartisan Taskforce for Combating Anti-Semitism, and recently appointed to the Council on the U.S. Holocaust Memorial Council by Speaker Ryan. She will be back shortly, but she wanted to convey to you that she appreciates your being here and your testimony.

I would also like to just recognize Ira Forman, who was the Special Envoy to Monitor and Combat Anti-Semitism from 2013 to 2016.

Thank you so very much, Mr. Special Envoy, for being here, for your work, which was greatly appreciated by all of us. And know that you will be invited—we want you to come and give your insights perhaps at the next hearing, when we have the administration here, as well, with the new Special Envoy.

I would like to now ask Ms. Burdett if you would proceed.

STATEMENT OF MS. STACY BURDETT, VICE PRESIDENT, GOVERNMENT RELATIONS, ADVOCACY, AND COMMUNITY ENGAGEMENT, ANTI-DEFAMATION LEAGUE

Ms. BURDETT. Thank you very much, Mr. Chairman, and thank you, Madam Ranking Member, for inviting me here, and thank you for your leadership in convening this hearing.

And thank you, Mr. Suozzi. We are all freshmen here. We are all learning new lessons. We are all taking on new commitments. And you don't have to chair a committee to make an impact on this issue. So you are honoring me with your time today.

I would like to request that my full statement and attachments be made part of the record.

Mr. SMITH. Without objection, so ordered.

Ms. BURDETT. Thank you.

And I would like to just take some time to highlight a couple of key lessons that I think can complement what my friends and colleagues are saying.

We have learned a lot from the moment that we are in, and we have to take those lessons very quickly and turn them into lessons that animate our actions.

Anti-Semitism is a global problem. You have heard from my colleague and friend Paul Goldenberg, no country is immune, not even a remarkable country like ours. And the fight for policies and institutions is one that we have to fight every day. The chairman knows from his work in the OSCE, vital democratic protections and freedoms, they are not self-executing.

And we are in that fight right now, and our success is extremely consequential, not just for Jewish communities but for America, for its moral leadership, for societies around the world.

And, Madam Ranking Member, for every community in the United States that feels a little more unwelcome or unsafe today, the fights against anti-Semitism and hate are inextricably connected. When we have fought anti-Semitism in America and around the world, everyone and their children sleep a little bit easier at night. So thank you for that important message.

I have appended to my testimony a map of this country that illustrates what probably is imprinted in Paul's mind every night when he goes to sleep, a map of where these threats are.

We know that conspiracy theories are taking center stage in everyone's political debate—ours, countries all over the world. And they can broadcast that hate. David Duke and the alt-right can go right into the palm of your hand and scare you right where you live; or engage in trolling and doxing, like what Paul described in Whitefish, Montana, where you post people's information publicly. And you don't even have to say anything, you don't have to threaten anything. You can just say, "Tell them how you feel. Tell these Jewish people how you feel. Don't do anything illegal." That is extremely personal, close to the bone.

And we have learned that these threats start online, but, boy, they move offline into the real world, where they are very dangerous.

ADL is increasing our investment in this area. We have just last week announced the opening of a new Center on Technology and Society that will be based in Silicon Valley. We have already been engaging with industry leaders in Europe, in the United States, all over the world, and using multilateral fora, international organizations that are the purview of this subcommittee, like UNESCO, like the U.N.'s Alliance of Civilization, like the Organization for Security and Cooperation in Europe. Those are fora where lawmakers and policymakers like you are networking with each other to adopt best practices, codes of conduct. We are networking in international fora with NGOs. And both sides of this table, we have our international fora, where we can band together to fight this cyber harassment.

My colleague also referenced a big data study that ADL released during the election campaign. And those 10 billion impressions of anti-Semitic tweets—I think we all were paying attention—they targeted about a dozen journalists, Jewish journalists, in ways that we know made those reporters stand up and say, I am going to give it a moment of thought before I cover a candidate or an individual in an honest way; it might not be worth it to me to be so harassed. So that gives us pause.

So the government has a primary responsibility to make people feel safe, to model good behavior, and to spotlight the problem. I have included 10 recommendations. I hope they are all easy. I want to just highlight a couple, because I think you are going to get a lot of good recommendations today.

America's human rights and democracy programs that former Special Envoy Ira Forman has expanded, enhanced, mobilized, energized, put them, as the chairman said, on steroids—those programs, they are part of our foreign affairs machinery, and they can't be effective on the cheap. Every single one of you is going to cast a vote about our foreign affairs budget, and I would like you to keep in mind that our ability to fight anti-Semitism around the world depends on having the resources to engage the world successfully.

I just want to highlight one other area, and this is in my recommendations as well. One of the most remarkable things we do as a country, when we report human rights violations in every country in the world, when we spotlight those problems, we are not only setting a moral marker, setting a tone that we hope other countries will follow, we do something vital, we lead by example. We have always done that. Our moral leadership deeply matters in this world and in this fight.

And when a monster goes to a Jewish cemetery in St. Louis to turn over 100-and-some heavy tombstones, that is a powerful attack on the presence of that community. Whether it is in Missouri or in Pennsylvania or in central Europe, you are saying: Your perpetuity, your children, your presence is offensive to people; be afraid.

And we want to make sure that not only are governments around the world reporting these incidents—please take a look at my second appendix. It is a scorecard of 57 countries, where, with the help of Rabbi Baker and Chairman Smith, we now have data in 57 OSCE countries.

But I want you to remember, please, one number: 3,441. Three thousand four hundred forty one. That is the number of American police departments that don't report any hate crime. When a monster comes to that cemetery, nobody tells the FBI. We don't know what is happening there.

Paul is correct, law enforcement does a remarkable job. We are a model for the world. But we have to fight for our standing as a country that leads by example.

And so, in California, all over the world, in Elizabeth, New Jersey, in Patterson, New Jersey, in Newark, there are just too many people there, too much diversity to believe that there were zero hate crimes in 2015.

So, for freshmen, for Mr. Suozzi, you can leave this chamber, and law enforcement in your State and in your district, they care very much what you think about the importance of making sure that we lead by example and that we bother to tell the FBI when people in our communities are targeted by hate.

I can't thank you all enough for your attention and for your leadership.

And I would like to make an additional request. Perhaps it might be helpful if I would enter into the record a list of cities in the United States with over 100,000 residents who either report zero hate crimes or don't bother to give an answer at all. That is a good followup item for every Member of this body.

Thank you very much.

[The prepared statement of Ms. Burdett follows:]

Anti-Defamation League®

Statement by Stacy Burdett

Vice President, Government Relations, Advocacy & Community Engagement

Before the

House Committee on Foreign Affairs

Subcommittee on Africa, Global Health, Global Human Rights, and International Organizations Hearing:

Anti-Semitism across Borders

March 22, 2017

On behalf of the Anti-Defamation League, I commend Chairman Smith, Ranking Member Bass, and the Members of the House Foreign Affairs Subcommittee on Africa, Global Health, Global Human Rights, and International Organizations for holding today's hearing on anti-Semitism across borders and for the ongoing effort of this subcommittee to keep the fight against anti-Semitism a priority human rights issue.

Anti-Semitism is a major concern for the Anti-Defamation League – not only because we are a Jewish community organization, but because anti-Semitism, the longest and most persistent form of prejudice, threatens security and democracy and poisons the health of a society as a whole. We view the fight against anti-Semitism today as enhancing and strengthening the fight against all forms of hatred and hate crime. Human rights are universal, and ADL was founded in a belief that safeguarding Jewish rights, or those of any targeted group, advances the cause of rights for everyone.

The Anti-Defamation League (ADL) was established in 1913 to "stop the defamation of the Jewish people and secure justice and fair treatment for all." ADL does not view defending the Jewish people and securing civil rights for others as an "either/or" choice. Rather it always has been a matter of "both/and." We strengthen our own safety and dignity when we fight for others, and fighting for others strengthens our cause.

This mission has driven ADL to become a leading resource on effective responses to violent bigotry, defending democratic ideals and protecting civil rights for all. Today, ADL carries out its mission through a network of 27 Regional Offices in the United States and abroad.

Anti-Semitic Harassment and Violence

Anti-Semitism is a form of hatred, mistrust, and contempt for Jews based on a variety of stereotypes and myths, and often invokes the belief that Jews have extraordinary influence with which they conspire to harm or control society. It can target Jews as individuals, as a group or as a people, or it can target the State of Israel as a Jewish entity. Criticism of Israel or Zionism is anti-Semitic when it uses anti-Jewish stereotypes or invokes anti-Semitic symbols and images, denies the Jewish right to self-determination, or holds Jews collectively responsible for actions of the State of Israel.

Today, overt anti-Jewish discrimination is not state-sponsored as it once was in many countries and it does not bar Jews from full participation in their society. Instead, in many regions, a Jew's right to live in security and to express his/her identity with dignity is threatened by an atmosphere of intimidation, harassment and violence against Jews and Jewish sites like schools, synagogues, shops and cemeteries. It is this everyday fear that prevents Jews in many places from being able to express who they are, to freely wear yarmulkes, Stars of David, or even T-shirts bearing Hebrew lettering or slogans.

Several factors affect the confidence level of Jews to live openly and freely as Jews, and those factors differ in emphasis in different communities. The Jewish communities in France and Hungary are both under significant threat, for instance, but the threats themselves differ significantly. These differ from, for example, South Africa or Argentina.

Key indicators of rising anti-Semitism are: (1) the degree of anti-Semitic attitudes held by the general population; (2) the number and nature of anti-Semitic incidents; (3) anti-Semitism in politics and media; and (4) the reaction of governments and civil society to these incidents. In 2014, ADL released a groundbreaking survey to establish for the first time comprehensive, data-based research of the level and intensity of anti-Jewish sentiment around the world. The ADL Global 100: An Index of Anti-Semitism surveyed 53,100 adults in 102 countries and territories and found that more than one-in-four adults, 26 percent of those surveyed, hold anti-Semitic attitudes. A follow-up to this survey was done in 2015 and found that although anti-Semitic attitudes dropped slightly in European countries such as France, Belgium, and Germany, concern about violence directed against Jews in those countries increased dramatically.

When Hate Comes Home

As recent desecrations of Jewish cemeteries in St. Louis, Philadelphia and Rochester, and the 165 bomb threats (as of 3/21/17) against Jewish institutions in the United States and Canada demonstrate, despite efforts to educate, raise awareness, and advocate, anti-Jewish attitudes and incidents in the United States remain a disturbing part of the American Jewish experience. See Appendix I for a map of where the threats have taken place.

The latest ADL Audit of Anti-Semitic Incidents found that in 2015, there were 941 anti-Semitic incidents, a three percent increase over the 912 incidents reported in 2014. The *Audit* included 56 cases of anti-Semitic assaults, a dramatic increase from the 36 reported in 2014; 508 anti-Semitic incidents of harassment, threats and events, a slight decrease from the 513 in 2014; and 377 cases of anti-Semitic vandalism, an increase from 363 in 2014.

Fringe anti-Semitic conspiracy theorists rarely miss an opportunity to exploit tragedies to promote their hatred of Jews, as they did blaming Jews for events ranging from coordinated terror attacks across Paris in November 2015 to the Sandy Hook Elementary School massacre in December 2012 to the 9/11 terrorist attacks. Some social media users responded by posting vehemently anti-Semitic messages on Twitter, making accusations similar to those of David Duke or Veterans Today, either blaming Jews themselves for perpetrating the attacks or Jewish control of a number of sectors in the U.S. for inspiring the attacks.

Cause for Concern Around the World

The challenges facing Jewish communities are diverse, even just within Europe. The numbers of documented anti-Semitic incidents in 2016, compared to 2015, were higher in the UK and lower in France, but both communities report increasing concerns about the mainstreaming of anti-Semitic political discourse. In Western Europe, security concerns continue to dominate, although there were no large-scale terror attacks on Jewish targets in 2016. In Central and Eastern Europe, media outlets like Radio Maryia in Poland, create a toxic atmosphere by broadcasting anti-Semitism. The rise of far-right groups, who may use the refugee crisis or economic distress to foment fear, scapegoating and bigotry, contributed to unease in some Jewish communities.

Sample Best Practice:
In May, ADL will host 10 European Jewish students – 19 and 20 year olds – from smaller communities in Europe for a training program on responding to anti-Semitism and anti-Israel bias. This "First Responders" program is co-sponsored by the European Jewish Congress and the Jewish Community of Oslo. The multiplier value of this program is already coming to bear. Two of the Norwegian students in last year's pilot program are conducting their own seminar this Sunday for non-Jewish Norwegian students to explain anti-Semitism to them and speak about anti-Semitism related to criticism of Israel.

In Latin America over the past few years, there has been a region-wide increase in anti-Semitic expressions and attacks directed at Jewish individuals and institutions, primarily via the internet and social media. Venezuela continues to be a country where state-endorsed anti-Semitism is systematic and affects government policies everyday life for Jews. Argentina, where the Jewish community has been target of infamous anti-Jewish terrorist attacks, continues to be the country with the greatest number of reported anti-Semitic incidents in the region. Smaller countries like Costa Rica and Uruguay, where anti-Semitism was practically negligible, are now facing new challenges. In Uruguay, for example, in March 2016, a Jewish businessman was stabbed to death by a man who said that "he killed a Jew following Allah's order."

Across the Middle East, anti-Semitic themes and conspiracy theories populate the print and broadcast media. For example, following the 2016 US presidential elections, editorial cartoons featured "Jews" as the real victor. In Iran, state-sponsored anti-Semitism continues to be a reality. The Islamic Republic's top officials espouse anti-Jewish and anti-Israel conspiracy theories, including Supreme Leader Khamenei who has referred to Israel as a "cancerous tumor" and expressed support for Palestinian violence to fight Israel's existence. And, in the spring of 2016 a "Holocaust Cartoon" contest was held, with the official sponsorship and support of the Iranian Ministry of Culture and Islamic Guidance.

Violent expressions of anti-Semitism, including encouragement of attacks against Jews and Jewish or Israeli institutions, have been at the core of propaganda distributed by Al Qaeda, ISIS, and other Islamic extremist terrorist groups for decades. In 2015, ADL's report, "Anti-Semitism: A Pillar of Islamic Extremist Ideology," describes the way in which terrorist organizations rely on depictions of a Jewish enemy to recruit followers, motivate adherents and draw attention to their cause.

Tackling Anti-Semitism Online

Online hate speech is global by nature. A call to kill Jews can be uploaded in the Middle East and watched around the world at any time. Proponents of hate inject anti-Semitic content, inferences and narratives into every platform from @killjews on Twitter, to a *Jewish Ritual Murder* page on Facebook, to a *Jews Did 9/11* video on YouTube to anti-Semitic memes to Stormfront.org, a multilingual racist website which has existed since the dawn of the Internet.

During the 2016 campaign, ADL documented a shocking level of anti-Semitic harassment targeting Jewish journalists on Twitter. ADL found a total of 2.6 million tweets containing anti-Semitic language shared on Twitter between August 2015 and July 2016. Those tweets had an estimated 10 billion impressions (reach), which helps reinforce and normalize previously taboo anti-Semitic language— on a massive scale.

ADL engages international organizations on the issue of cyberbullying in for a like UNESCO's conference in Seoul, South Korea on cyberbullying, or by reporting the online harassment of refugees and migrants to stakeholders in the UN's Alliance of Civilizations. ADL is involved in several NGO global networks to combat cyberhate and cyberbullying. Governments should be banding together in their multilateral bodies to do the same.

The ADL Cyber-Safety Action Guide, available at www.adl.org/cybersafetyguide, features tabs where visitors may access information on submitting complaints and reporting hate speech to the major online companies, including Facebook, YouTube and Twitter. The ADL resource links users to each company's cyber-bullying and harassment policies and terms of service, as well as links directly to online complaint forms.

For each Internet company, the ADL resource identifies:
- The company's general hate speech policy, if one exists;
- Information on the company's cyber-bullying and harassment policy;
- Links to pages and/or an e-mail address where users may lodge a formal complaint.

Because of the enormous volume of uploaded content, companies typically rely on users to bring offensive speech to their attention. This tool enables internet users to better use their voices. Companies such as Amazon, AT&T, Comcast, eBay, Facebook, Google, Instagram, LinkedIn, Pinterest, Tumblr., Twitter, Vimeo, and YouTube are represented and many have spoken in support of this effort. To address the growing problem of online hate in Latin America, ADL released the *Cyber Safety Action Guide* in Spanish.

In 2014, ADL published "Best Practices for Responding to Cyberhate," the outcome of months of discussions and deliberations by an industry Working Group on Cyberhate convened by ADL. ADL shared the guide with the European Commission to serve as a guide for its cyberhate discussions with industry. Those EC negotiations culminated in a Code of Conduct agreement between the Commission and industry. ADL has also been invited to present the Best Practices document in France at a meeting organized by the French Jewish community organization, CRIF, with representatives from the French government, law enforcement, the leadership of companies like Google, Facebook, Twitter, and key NGOs.

Sample Best Practice:
Next month, ADL will convene a forum to bring together senior global policy leaders from Google, Facebook, Microsoft and other technology companies and Jewish community leaders from around the world. Over a dozen Jewish leaders from Europe, Latin America, Canada, and South Africa will hear from industry policymakers and ADL experts about advances in combating cyberhate, remaining challenges, and the will have an important opportunity to pose questions directly to decision makers in the industry.

Anti-Semitism Doesn't Exist, or Grow, in a Vacuum
Anti-Semitism flourishes in the context of, and often in conjunction with, persecution of other groups on the basis of religion, gender, sexual orientation, gender identity, race, or ethnicity. In order to effectively fight anti-Semitism and bigotry, no one group should fight hatred in isolation.

This year in particular xenophobic and hateful rhetoric dominated political discourse in several European and Eurasian countries, and this rhetoric was often matched with hate-inspired violence. For example, in some countries, the rise of far-right groups, who may use the refugee crisis or economic distress to foment fear, scapegoating and bigotry, contributed to a wave of xenophobic violence. Perhaps most stunning is the case of the neo-Nazi Golden Dawn party in Greece, which polled third in national elections in September 2015 even though its entire leadership is on trial for its role in dozens of violent attacks— including murders—targeting migrants and others[1].

Sample Best Practice
Through ADL's Partners Against Anti-Semitism (PAAS) program, diverse members of civil society in Hungary & Greece, from Jewish, LGBT, Roma, migrant, and other targeted communities launched advocacy efforts against anti-Semitism and hate. In each country, activists worked together in the first coalition of its kind to directly address anti-Semitism and bigotry in Europe where the problem is severe and efforts to counteract it are oft-met with public indifference or resistance. ADL equipped participants with concrete strategies for confronting anti-Semitism at all levels of politics, civil society, and community life and funded projects to expand public awareness and engagement by a broader range of stakeholders to reject anti-Semitism expressed in the public discourse and fomented by political parties.

---

[1] *Scorecard on Hate Crime Response in the OSCE Region, Anti-Defamation League and Human Rights First (2016). See appendix II. Also available at:* http://www.humanrightsfirst.org/sites/default/files/ADL-HRF-HateCrimes-Scorecard-11.28.16.final_.pdf

Governments bear the primary responsibility to ensure that Jews are afforded the same rights as others to live in security and with dignity in their communities. Whether it is espoused by hate groups on the margins or political parties garnering support in elections, governments and civic leaders can mobilize political will to reject anti-Semitism and its messengers and to use human rights and anti-discrimination instruments related to anti-Semitism and intolerance.

Recommendations for Action

Below are recommendations for Congress to institutionalize a systemic, comprehensive strategy against anti-Semitism and other forms of violent bigotry.

1. **Start by using our government's own bully pulpit to speak out.** Political leaders have the most immediate and significant opportunity to set the tone of a national response to an anti-Semitic incident, an anti-Semitic party or an anti-Semitic parliamentarian. Nothing gives a greater sense of security than seeing anti-Semitism and other forms of bigotry publicly rejected. This signals that the government takes seriously the impact of this climate on the community.

2. **Prioritize combating anti-Semitism and hate crimes on bilateral and multilateral organization agendas.** The U.S. should let our allies know that addressing anti-Semitism and hate crime is a core part of our bilateral agenda and within multilateral institutions, including the United Nations. Congress has a central role to play in promoting this emphasis both within the State Department and in your own bilateral contacts and outreach to foreign officials.

3. **Monitor and Spotlight the Problem:** Sunlight is the best disinfectant. U.S. reporting on anti-Semitism as a human rights and religious freedom issue is an indispensable tool in spotlighting the problem and a tool for U.S. diplomacy. Congress has been a vital driver of expanding and improving U.S. reporting on anti-Semitism and other human rights violations and your support for the State Department's annual country reports on human rights and on international religious freedom matters.

4. Members of the Subcommittee can **join the 115th House Bi-Partisan Taskforce for Combating Anti-Semitism,** a forum to collectively denounce anti-Semitic incidents and to support enforcement and prevention efforts. The Taskforce also provides a legislative platform to promote Holocaust remembrance and to mobilize leadership against hatred at home and around the world.

5. **Urge the swift appointment of a strong Special Envoy to Monitor and Combat Anti-Semitism** and support robust work of the Special Envoy's Office. This will ensure that the U.S. maintains a specialized focus on anti-Semitism and a dedicated effort to mobilize the arsenal of U.S. diplomatic tools to respond.

6. **Equip U.S. Diplomats with Training** to Sustain Improvement in U.S. Reporting and Response. Anti-Semitism is a continuously mutating phenomenon that is not always easy to discern. The Special Envoy expanded training on anti-Semitism in the State Department's Foreign Service Institute to give diplomats the understanding and tools to recognize anti-Semitism and the contemporary forms it takes. The Foreign Service Institute course on "Promoting Human Rights and Democracy" should consistently include such training.

7. **Congress and the Administration should have visible contact with Jewish communities that feel under siege**. Every trip is an opportunity to elevate the fight against anti-Semitism. Let your counterparts abroad know that addressing anti-Semitism and hate crime is a core concern. Members can emphasize this in own bilateral contacts and outreach to foreign officials.

8. **Combating anti-Semitism and hate crimes should be part of the full array of human rights and democracy programming**. Training and assistance programs should include a focus on improving the policing and prosecution of anti-Semitic and other hate crimes. Much more can be done to leverage the international visitor program as well as trainings geared toward law enforcement such as the Department of Justice OPDAT and ICITAP programs or training delivered through U.S. International Law Enforcement Academies (ILEA), that reach governmental and law enforcement audiences around the world.

9. **Support a robust foreign affairs budget** to make U.S. efforts against global anti-Semitism, hate crime, and terror possible. Our ability to fight global anti-Semitism and extremism hinges on having the resources to successfully engage in the world, and to help prevent unstable areas from becoming breeding grounds for violent extremism.

10. **Lead by Example**: Strengthen the fight against anti-Semitism and intolerance at home. Congress has been instrumental in calling on countries to monitor and combat anti-Semitism on the international stage. Legislators also have the ability to strengthen America's efforts to address and prevent anti-Semitism and hate crime here at home. Leading by example requires helping law enforcement, communities, and schools implement effective hate crimes prevention programs and activities. Learn about what law enforcement agencies in your Congressional district are doing to report hate crime and whether any of the 3,441 police agencies that don't participate in this reporting are in your district.

Appendix I.

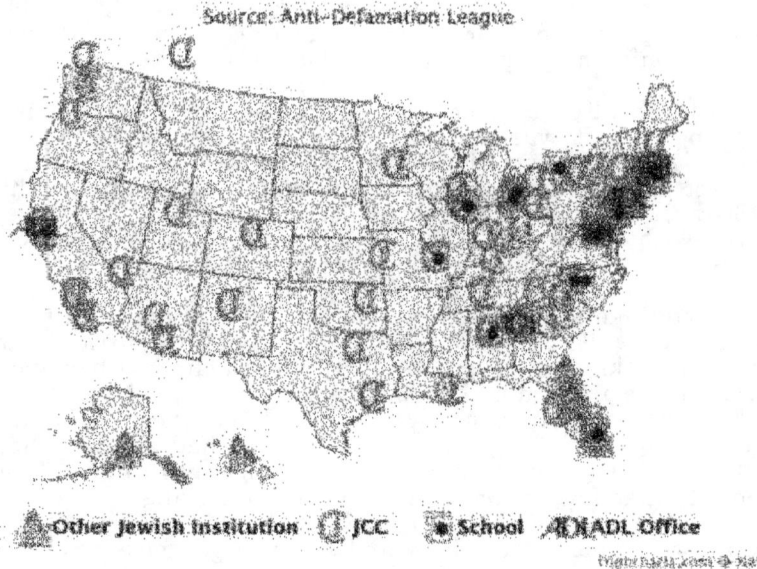

Bomb Threats Against Jewish Institutions, 2017

Source: Anti-Defamation League

Mr. SMITH. Thank you, Ms. Burdett.

Thank you, Ms. Bass.

I would like to now yield to Rabbi Baker.

And, without objection, your last request will be made a part of the record.

STATEMENT OF RABBI ANDREW BAKER, PERSONAL REPRESENTATIVE ON COMBATING ANTI-SEMITISM, OFFICE OF THE CHAIRPERSON-IN-OFFICE, ORGANIZATION FOR SECURITY AND CO-OPERATION IN EUROPE

Rabbi BAKER. Chairman Smith, thank you for this opportunity to testify, but thank you and your colleagues for the leadership you have shown, really, over a very long period of time. I think we all know and you cited earlier, the U.S. effort in the case of the OSCE, but in other areas, to get countries to focus on this problem, to really step up and address it was critical, starting with that first OSCE conference and all the various other things that have followed.

It should also be noted that before the U.S. Government really got engaged, it was you and other Members of Congress that pushed an administration, often not because of opposition to the subject but worried about complications, difficulty within the OSCE, the consensus process, and other things.

So, without the advocacy here, I think much of what we have been able to do would not have succeeded. And it is a lesson that we need to keep in front of us even as we go forward.

I would like for the record that you accept my written testimony. And here I will simply try to highlight what I have tried to present more as a kind of progress report and, again, with a particular focus on the problem in Europe.

Security, as you have already heard, has been a paramount issue. And the fact is, for many years, we had a real difficulty in getting governments to recognize the challenges, the very need for security that Jewish communities were witnessing.

It had much to do, I think, with the advocacy of many of the organizations represented here and so on to get governments to pay attention. But, at the same time, and tragically, it was only after some of these terrorist attacks, deaths in Brussels, in Paris, in Copenhagen, that governments at least began to recognize the problem.

But doing something was another issue altogether. And we have seen success, but we know it is only partial.

Congressman Schneider referenced France earlier. It is true that, because of what we saw there, the government stepped forward. It literally mobilized the military. And so every school, every synagogue, every community building was protected. And incidents went down last year, and in significant numbers. Even, it appears, the number of Jews leaving France, a real problem itself, has decreased.

But the Jewish community knows, and we have now seen, this was not a permanent step, that security is no longer there, the government can't afford to do this, and, in fact, terrorist threats are present throughout the country. So what will happen? How to keep that attention, how to keep that mobilization is still not certain.

In Sweden, which has the largest Jewish community in Scandinavia, we have seen them begin to mobilize, recognize the security needs are real. We have pushed governments to come forward with funding. In effect, the mere practice of your religious freedom is challenged if people are fearful of going out in public, being physically identified as Jews. In some cases, simply attending a Jewish event has caused people to second-guess and think about what they are doing.

So, in Stockholm and Malmo, there are new efforts. Paul and I recall particularly visiting Malmo and, at the time, seeing the embattled nature of that Jewish community. There is now security support. We didn't have that before. There are more funds going to support community institutions. But more is still needed. And the communities in both places will still tell us, yes, we have some help, but the governments, which have begun to mobilize, need to do more.

In a place like the UK, we have probably the best example of good cooperation between a Jewish community and government authorities. The UK's Jewish Community Security Trust has been monitoring incidents, and has, in fact, been directly training police. And there is, not only in this relationship, something that has provided a real security net for the Jewish community, they are now being asked to help assist in providing security for other religious communities in the UK. It is a model, and it is one we have cited before and deserves recognizing still again.

It is also work, as we know, the problem not only with cyber hate but of conveying information through the Internet and through social media and finding some very good ways of using that to alert a Jewish community when there are problems or when there are steps that are being taken.

And, finally, the OSCE's ODIHR has been implementing, developing a multi-year program known as Words Into Action specifically to focus on problems of anti-Semitism, with security being one of them. With significant funds coming from the German Government, the first measure they will take is producing a guideline, a security toolkit, if you will, on what governments, what NGOs, what different authorities should be doing when it comes to Jewish community security. This should be presented later this spring, first in Europe, but we certainly hope they will come here and we will have an opportunity to share what their recommendations are here in the United States.

Turning to a second issue, we have made efforts to convey the importance of having a clear and comprehensive definition of anti-Semitism. This goes back, as you know, over a decade. It may have been when the first studies were done in the European Union in 2003 and 2004; even the monitors conducting those surveys didn't have a full appreciation of anti-Semitism and what it was. Yes, maybe they understood hatred, prejudice, and discrimination toward Jews, but anti-Semitism presenting itself through conspiracy theories about Jews, anti-Semitism through the vehicle of Holocaust denial, and, as you cited in referencing Natan Sharansky, understanding how Israel can itself be a target or a form of anti-Semitism, as when it is declared of racist endeavor, when its very existence is challenged, or when analogies are drawn to the Nazi treatment of Jews. This is not criticism, it is anti-Semitism.

And we have had success in getting governments, in getting organizations to recognize the value of a comprehensive definition, starting with that EUMC working definition a decade ago, and now looking to individual countries to employ it. Our own Government and the office of the Special Envoy has used a version of that definition. With great success last year—and considerable kudos to my colleague Mark Weitzman—the IHRA, the International Holocaust Remembrance Alliance, essentially took that definition and managed to secure its adoption for use by IHRA and its 31 member countries.

With that in mind, the OSCE chair last year, German Foreign Minister, now President, Frank-Walter Steinmeier, said he wanted to secure the adoption by the OSCE for use in the OSCE of this definition. It was a considerable hurdle to get 57 countries to agree by consensus. Coming down to the wire in Hamburg, as you know, we ultimately got 56 of those 57 countries to agree. Only one, the Russian Federation, stood in the way for reasons I can go into later if you are interested. They were more excuses; they weren't legitimate reasons.

We very much hope it will be possible, changing dynamics perhaps, that during this calendar year, we could get the Russians to come onboard and, with the assistance of the now Austrian OSCE chair-in-office, try to push for that adoption in December 2017.

In the meantime, the UK Government has formally adopted this definition. We have managed to get Justice Ministers in Germany and Austria to say they will use it in training judges and prosecutors. We have even a formal statement by all of the EU countries within the OSCE endorsing this. So we hope more steps can be taken to put it into use.

I will turn to a third area. It is one that has been with us, but, in fact, it is flaring up yet again, and that is the question of balancing principles of religious freedom with maybe more secular forces in society. And I speak now about the elemental practices for Jews and for Muslims—they go back really to biblical times—of ritual circumcision and of ritual slaughter. They really are elemental to practicing religion today, but they have been under attack. Animal rights activists and children's rights advocates, maybe with genuine, legitimate motives, but they would seek to ban this practice of slaughter and limit the ability to circumcise our youth, our infants.

In this process, Jews now have to defend something they have been doing literally for centuries. It may not be in its initial intent an anti-Semitic campaign, but it surely is often in its result. By the way, it also links Jews and Muslims together. And so, where there have been some success, it has really depended on an alliance as both communities confronting this problem together.

Finally—and with this, I will close—we have to recognize there is still great unease at a very uncertain political climate when we look across the European continent. We see the success of right-wing, nationalist, xenophobic parties and movements, in some cases winning at the ballot box, finding their way into parliaments, even threatening, as we have seen in a couple of countries, to ascend to serious positions, such as the office of President.

In many cases, these are parties and movements that are virulently anti-immigrant, anti-Muslim, anti-Roma, but anti-Semitism has also been a significant part of them. And Jews do not feel comfortable even if it appears that the first target is someone else. In fact, as we have learned here in America, as has already been stated, I think our ability to combat anti-Semitism, to feel safe and secure, is part of the larger fight to combat racism, discrimination, and xenophobia across the board.

Having said that, Europe has some special challenges today. There are significant numbers of Arabs and Muslims, many more coming in as part of refugees and migrants from north Africa and from the Middle East. Many of them have attitudes, come with, frankly, sentiments and views that are anti-Israel and anti-Jewish, and also in many cases anti-Western.

The societies that have received these people, also that have had some difficulty in assimilating and integrating those who have come before them. They need to recognize this and try and step up and do more. The fact is Jewish communities have often confronted this significant increase in incidents of harassment or attack coming largely from parts of these communities. Not all governments are willing to confront this with a clear-eyed approach. And if they don't, they are not going to really be successful in figuring out strategies to deal with it in the short-term when it comes to security, but long-term when it comes to educational efforts and the like.

So here, too, we need to keep focus on what is in front of us, I think, to recognize we have had success, we have attention. We need to keep the support and the moral focus here in America to really assist us in this continuing combat, this continuing battle that we are waging across the ocean in Europe.

So thank you again for this opportunity.

[The prepared statement of Rabbi Baker follows:]

RABBI ANDREW BAKER
Personal Representative of the OSCE Chairperson-in-Office on Combating Anti-Semitism
AJC Director of International Jewish Affairs
COMMITTEE ON FOREIGN AFFAIRS
Subcommittee on Africa, Global Health, Global Human Rights, and International
Organizations
HEARING: ANTI-SEMITISM ACROSS BORDERS
March 22, 2017

JEWISH COMMUNITY SECURITY

We have spent much energy trying to convince governments of the special security challenges that Jewish communities in Europe face and then pressing them to take action to address these problems. Of particular note in this effort was the OSCE Expert Conference on Jewish Community Security in Berlin in 2012, in which Jewish community leaders and law enforcement officials described the situation and offered some best practice examples.[1]

Eventually governments came to recognize the seriousness of the situation. I would like to think that this was due to the successful advocacy efforts on my part and on the part of other individuals and organizations. But in reality we were surely helped by the tragic events of terrorist attacks in Paris, Brussels and Copenhagen. No longer were governments able to ignore the situation.

They have responded, and that is good news. But problems still remain. Governments have taken different approaches, and some only in stop-gap measures.

The French government mobilized the military to protect Jewish schools and other institutions, an unprecedented step to offer security to Europe's largest Jewish community. There is little doubt that this resulted in a significant reduction in anti-Semitic incidents reported last year and probably also in the decline of French Jews leaving the country for Israel or elsewhere. However, no one expected that this would be a permanent measure. And in the face of more general terrorist attacks and threats, security forces are being repositioned.

The Jewish community in Sweden reported that its government stepped up its activities following the terror attack on the synagogue in nearby Copenhagen. The Stockholm community had been spending a quarter of its budget for security needs, and it faced a variety of road blocks even in implementing its own measures. By way of example, positioning security cameras on the streets in front of the synagogue and community centers was deemed a violation of privacy protections. In the city of Malmö there had been a dramatic number of anti-

---

[1] "Summary Report of the Expert Conference on Addressing the Security Needs of Jewish Communities in the OSCE Region: Challenges and Good Practices." 13 June 2012. Berlin, Germany. http://www.osce.org/odihr/105253?download=true. Accessed March 2017.

Semitic incidents— by all accounts mostly stemming from the city's large immigrant community— leading to a steady emigration of Jewish families.

I visited Stockholm and Malmö again this past September. The government is providing funds to upgrade the security of Jewish buildings—and those of other religious and ethnic communities—and deserves commendation for this. But policies that limit the amount that can be spent on each building—a seemingly fair approach in the abstract—are a special burden to the Stockholm Jewish community. Much of its activity takes place in a recently-constructed community center that combines a day school with a café, communal offices, a kosher market and meeting spaces. The costs necessary to provide the needed security enhancements—not envisioned in the initial design—far exceed the per-building subsidies that are offered.

The Malmö Jewish community reports that it now has received funding to pay for a full-time security professional. After repeated anti-Semitic attacks on the community's rabbi, one perpetrator was finally apprehended and prosecuted. However, they also note the lack of coordination and communication between them and police and intelligence agencies. When I brought this up at a meeting with the city's own security chief, he expressed his own frustration at receiving very little essential information from the national authorities.

By all accounts the United Kingdom offers the most successful relationship between the Jewish community and government authorities in dealing with security concerns. The community's security arm, the Community Security Trust (CST), works closely with police authorities in nearly all respects.[2] They share data and a unified approach to monitor incidents; they are involved in the development of teaching manuals for police cadets and in their ongoing education program; and they are now collaborating in providing training in security and data collection for other faith communities.[3] The CST and government authorities have also devised new methods to alert Jewish community members of impending dangers or special measures by linking these messages to key topics and phrases on Internet search engines.

Finally, I want to cite the work of ODIHR and its Words into Action project which is now in the final stages of preparing a comprehensive practical guideline for government authorities on Jewish community security.[4] This "security toolkit"—the result of extensive consultations with police professionals and NGO representatives—will be presented later this spring. It offers recommended practices and useful examples, and I very much hope that it will be taken onboard by the OSCE participating States.

WORKING DEFINITION OF ANTI-SEMITISM

---

[2] https://cst.org.uk/about-cst/police-partnership

[3] "A Guide to Fighting Hate Crimes: A CST Publication. "Community Security Trust https://cst.org.uk/public/data/file/1/0/Hate-Crime-booklet.pdf. Accessed March 2017.

[4] http://www.osce.org/project/words-into-action-to-address-anti-semitism

Ten years have passed since the European Monitoring Centre on Racism and Xenophobia (EUMC) issued its Working Definition on Antisemitism.[5] This is a comprehensive definition that, together with examples, provides an important guide for civil society monitors and government officials alike in understanding the various manifestations of anti-Semitism. At its core anti-Semitism is a hatred of and prejudice against Jews but it also presents itself in conspiracies about Jews, in Holocaust denial, and in ways relating to the State of Israel. It is a useful tool in helping police recognize anti-Semitic hate crimes and in assisting prosecutors and judges in their work. Without its guidance we have seen how real attacks on Jewish targets are still dismissed as politically-motivated incidents.

Last year the International Holocaust Remembrance Alliance (IHRA), consisting of thirty-one member governments, adopted the Working Definition at its plenary session in Romania.[6] Also last year the OSCE Chair-in-Office, German Foreign Minister Frank-Walter Steinmeier, sought to secure the official adoption of the same definition at the OSCE Ministerial Meeting in Hamburg in December. As those who were present know, effectively 56 of the 57 participating States were prepared to accept the draft decision on this presented by the Chairmanship. In the end, only the Russian Federation stood in the way of its adoption—by raising questionable reservations and proposing last minute changes that would alter the essential meaning of the decision. I very much hope that under the current Austrian Chairmanship the OSCE will again seek adoption of the Working Definition. Obviously, we will need to make new efforts to secure the Russian endorsement of an acceptable draft decision if we are to succeed.

In the meantime we can cite several important examples of the endorsement and use of the definition:

- The UK Government, following a recommendation by the Parliamentary Home Affairs Committee, has formally adopted the definition for use in that country.[7]

- On January 26, 2017 the collective EU Member States bloc in the OSCE Permanent Council issued a statement that noted their support for the OSCE adopting of the Working Definition—the first written endorsement by the European Union.[8]

---

[5] "EUMC Working Definition of Antisemitism." European Parliament Working Group on Antisemitism. http://www.antisem.eu/projects/eumc-working-definition-of-antisemitism/. Accessed March 2017.

[6] https://www.holocaustremembrance.com/sites/default/files/press_release_document_antise mitism.pdf

[7] Walker, Peter. "UK adopts antisemitism definition to combat hate crime against Jews." The Guardian. 11 December 2016. https://www.theguardian.com/society/2016/dec/12/antisemitism-definition-government-combat-hate-crime-jews-israel. Accessed March 2017.

[8] "Déclaration de l'UE en réponse au Président de l'Alliance Internationale pour la mémoire de l'Holocauste." OSCE Conseil Permanent No 1129 Vienne, 26 janvier 2017. http://www.osce.org/fr/pc/296796?download=true, p.2. Accessed March 2017.

- The Justice Ministers of Austria and Germany have each announced that the definition would be part of the materials used in the training of new prosecutors and judges.

- The ODIHR security guidelines (mentioned above) will also include the full definition.

RELIGIOUS FREEDOM AND RITUAL PRACTICES

We are also mindful of efforts in a number of European states to restrict or ban altogether the longstanding ritual practices of circumcision and animal slaughter. These practices—*brit milah* and *sh'chita* in Hebrew—have been elemental requirements of Jewish observance since Biblical times. Prohibiting them would represent a genuine challenge to the continued viability of Jewish life in these countries.

Proponents of these bans are most often children's rights advocates or animal rights activists. There is little doubt that support also comes from a growing anti-Muslim animus in these countries, as Islam also mandates its own version of male circumcision and ritual slaughter. Additionally, the inherent principle of religious freedom which we hold in such high regard in the United States may be viewed differently in Europe with its own legacy of religious domination in state affairs.

Jewish communities have already accommodated themselves to some restrictions. A number of countries prohibit religious slaughter altogether. In some cases this legislation dates back decades and was originally enacted with a clear anti-Semitic intent to discourage Jews from settling there. For the moment there are still no restrictions on the importation of kosher meat. But as prohibitions increase, even this may be challenged. In some countries legislation imposing conditions on the practice of infant circumcision, such as requiring the presence of medical professionals has been enacted with the agreement of the Jewish community. But rather than ending the debate, there are new calls to ban the practice altogether.

Ironically, with all the anti-Semitic restrictions that accompanied Jewish life in Europe over the centuries, Jews were generally left alone to carry out these internal acts of religious observance as they saw fit. Until now there was no need to make a public defense, let alone to devise a compelling argument to a largely secular public.

In the face of this, there are some positive developments including growing Muslim-Jewish cooperation in countering these efforts. There are also plans now for ODIHR to convene a meeting on religious freedom and ritual practice early this summer that will highlight these efforts and seek to raise awareness to the challenges posed to religious life in Europe.

UNCERTAIN POLITICAL CLIMATE

I cannot leave unspoken a general concern and unease at the increasing support for right-wing, populist and xenophobic political parties in much of Europe. The ideology and agenda of these parties are primarily stoking fears of Muslims, Roma and Sinti, and recent waves of migrants primarily from the Middle East. But European Jews themselves also recognize that these movements will not view them kindly. Many of these parties' supporters if not the leaders themselves are openly anti-Semitic. Marine Le Pen, the Presidential candidate of France's National Front Party, has already indicated that Jews must "do their part" in her call for banning the Muslim headscarf by removing their *kippot* in public too.[9] Even though in some countries the worst fears of their success—e.g., presidential elections in Austria and parliamentary elections in the Netherlands—may not have been realized, their potency cannot be discounted.

European Jewish leaders have so far largely maintained a policy of non-communication with these parties and their leaders, even as some of them are actively courting Jewish voters. They are also seeking with some limited success meetings with Israeli leaders and potential Jewish interlocutors in the United States. By most accounts the goal is one of "koshering" their candidacy rather than genuinely excising the anti-Semitism that is inherent in their ideology.

We need to be clear-eyed in confronting and combating anti-Semitism, which manifests itself on both the right and the left. Many incidents of anti-Semitism come from segments of the Muslim communities in Europe, and governments are not always willing to acknowledge this. There can be little doubt that many of the newly-arriving refugees and migrants have brought with them to Europe the strongly anti-Jewish and anti-Israel sentiments that are so prevalent in their home countries. We cannot excuse this or ignore it or worse still allow it to be "balanced" by anti-Zionist proponents who would blame Israel and absolve these individuals.

At the same time, if the essential lesson of the long and vibrant chapter of Jewish life in America has taught us anything, it is that we are most secure in a society that is protective of all its minorities, appreciative of diversity and pluralism, and committed to eradicating racial, ethnic and religious discrimination. Surely what is true here—and we may need some reminders these days—also holds true for Europe.

---

[9] "Marine Le Pen: French Jews Should Sacrifice Yarmulke In Struggle Against Radical Islam." Jewish Telegraphic Agency. 6 February 2017. http://www.jta.org/2017/02/06/news-opinion/world/marine-le-pen-french-jews-should-sacrifice-yarmulke-in-struggle-against-radical-islam. Accessed March 2017.

Mr. SMITH. Thank you, Rabbi Baker, for that very extensive set of recommendations and the overview that you have provided us. And, without objection, your full statement—and this goes for all of our distinguished witnesses—and any attachments you would like to make a part of the record, so ordered.

Mr. Weitzman?

STATEMENT OF MR. MARK WEITZMAN, DIRECTOR OF GOVERNMENT AFFAIRS, SIMON WIESENTHAL CENTER

Mr. WEITZMAN. Thank you very much, Chairman Smith. I would like to begin by expressing my thanks and appreciation to you for your leadership in Congress and internationally, as well as for your personal activism on this issue, which we know has extended beyond just the legislative field but really to going out and intervening in cases directly. And your leadership is much appreciated.

I also want to thank the ranking member and the members of the subcommittee. And as a fellow New Yorker, my appreciation to Mr. Suozzi for his remarks and his presence on this issue as well. Anti-Semitism today is no longer limited to verbal expressions of hate. It is fueled by the stream of propaganda that radical Islamists put out online and the financial/political contributions to this campaign that come from some Muslim states and organiza- tions. An increasing number of terrorists have translated words into action and assaulted and murdered Jews throughout Europe and targeted Jewish institutions in Europe and the U.S. They have been joined in recent years and recent months by members of the radical right, extremists coming from all aspects of society and fringes of society, who have targeted Jews as their primary target. Continuing almost 20 years of efforts, next week the Simon Wiesenthal Center will be releasing its Digital Terrorism and Hate Electronic Report of extremism and anti-Semitism on the Internet, which includes grading the social media companies. We see that there is a frequent correlation between the amounts of propaganda and extremism and hate that come out online and the surge in radicalization and terrorism that often follow.

However, I would like to focus my remarks here on something that is somewhat different, and it is an aspect of political anti-Sem- itism, especially Holocaust distortion, that we can now see in grow- ing circles of Western democracy and Western democratic coun- tries.

To focus on one country in particular as a prime example of this, I would like to turn my attention to what is happening in Poland currently, where we have high-ranking officials, such as the Min- ister of Defense, who has in the past accepted the possibility that the classic text of anti-Semitism, the "Protocols of the Elders of Zion," are perhaps, in fact, true. And he claimed that "experience shows that there are such groups in Jewish circles." Two other ministers have declined to condemn the Protocols.

A prominent extremist Catholic radio station that has been con- demned by the Vatican for anti-Semitism and by the State Depart- ment as one of Europe's most blatantly anti-Semitic media venues continues to find favor in government circles, having received grants totaling millions of dollars over the past year, and even had a postage stamp recently issued in its honor.

Some of the quotes from people, the head of the radio station and commentators on the station, include: "The U.S. media and entertainment industry are dependent on the Jewish lobby. It is similar to the Stalinist terror, which was organized and implemented by Jewish communism." That speaker recently toured and spoke in New York, New Jersey, and Massachusetts in an effort to raise money and continue spreading the message of hate, not just locally but internationally.

The director of the Polish Institute in Berlin was recently fired for allegedly giving too much attention to Jewish subjects.

And, finally and perhaps most importantly, an amendment to a law that is being proposed in the Polish Parliament claims that whoever publicly claims, contrary to historical facts, the Polish nation or Polish state's responsibility or partial responsibility for Nazi crimes can be criminalized with a potential 3-year sentence. That means, in effect, that anybody who refers in a conversation, in writing, in research to murder of Jews during the Holocaust period by Poles has potentially committed a criminal act and can be sentenced to up to 3 years in prison.

I went to the files, the archives of the U.S. Holocaust Memorial Museum and just picked out three witness testimonies, survivor testimonies of survivors. And these are in my written remarks. And these survivors all testified to their experience where they found that the local population had been more deadly than the Nazis.

And for all sorts of reasons, and this is found in many cases throughout occupied Europe, through the Baltics, through other countries in Eastern and central Europe, this is not an uncommon experience. But those survivors, in the twilight of their years now can be found liable and sentenced for just recalling what happened to them and giving their impressions of that. And this is now potentially entering into law into Poland.

It will also have a greatly chilling effect on future research as well as freedom of speech in that country, where young scholars may be inhibited from even studying the Holocaust, people may be inhibited from publishing their research and their findings, and it is an attempt to essentially legislate history for political purposes. The prime focus of that has been Princeton professor, Jan Gross, whose remarks in an interview he gave to the German newspaper last year have been potentially seen as falling in violation of one of these types of laws. Charges were investigated and considered being brought. The first prosecutor in the case declined to bring charges. The superior reopened the investigation in what appears to be, again, a politically motivated effort.

Poland is not the only case. It was, perhaps, the most acute, but it is not, by far, the only case. The Ukraine has passed a similar law about anyone shaming the reputation of the fighters to Ukrainian independence, who include the partisan units that are responsible for murdering 100,000 Poles and tens of thousands of Jews.

In Russia, a law that forbids publication of what they described as falsehoods about the Soviet Union's role during World War II, has been used to convict the journalist who wrote, "The Communists Germans jointly invaded Poland sparking up World War II. That is, communism and Nazism closely collaborated."

As we know it is an historical fact that in September 1939, Poland was invaded on both sides by both those countries. Yet, to state that in Putin's Russia, now appears to be against the law.

In Croatia, the Jewish community has felt compelled to boycott official Holocaust commemorations over the past 2 years. A former Minister of Culture in Croatia embraced the Ustase, the Croatian collaborators, defended their actions in articles that he published, and was photographed in his younger days wearing the Ustase hat, and screened a film in the Jasenovac concentration camp that minimized the number of victims casting doubt on the authenticity of historical accounts of what happened in that camp.

Recently, plaques have been put in front of the camp with Ustase slogans, leading to the boycott for the second year by the Jewish community.

In Hungary, a proposed Holocaust museum was to be directed by a woman who has written articles with anti-Semitic themes in them. And the content was highly questionable. Statues were proposed to figures who collaborated with the Nazis, including one such figure, an historian, who, as a minister in the Hungarian Government and is a member of Parliament introduced the Hungarian version of the Nuremberg laws, stripping Jews of their right to protections of citizenship and opened the way to the eventual deportation and murder of almost 450,000 Jews.

Writers who had collaborated with the Nazis and written anti-Semitic works, were inserted into the school curriculum. A number of other issues went on to the point, again, where the Jewish community felt compelled to boycott the official commemorations of Hungarian Holocaust remembrance.

Fortunately, there has been some successful pushback on this. The IHRA, the International Holocaust Remembrance Alliance, has intervened both in Hungary and in the Polish issue. I participated as part of a four-member IHRA delegation that went to Poland to discuss this with the Polish Government in December. We are still waiting to hear positive results in Poland.

But in Hungary, through the International Holocaust Remembrance Alliance, through the direct intervention of Chairman Smith, who wrote a pivotal letter to Prime Minister Orban about the statues, through the efforts of Special Envoy Forman in the State Department, the Hungarian Government, the Prime Minister of Hungary, announced that they would not erect any more statues. They would hold off on the statues. They have held off on continuing work on the museum, saying that they would only put the final exhibits in—the museum was built and currently exists as a shell, but they would only put the exhibits in with the approval of the local Jewish community, as well as international experts. And, in many ways, that shows the power of the international body and the United States that work on these issues to intervene positively on it.

But this is some of the background to the American Jewish community's consternation to the White House statement regarding the January 27 on the Holocaust that omitted mention of Jews. Even a mistake seen in the context of this background can be used by people with bad intentions.

And as one crude example, last week, the Seattle synagogue was vandalized with the slogan, "The Holocaust is fake history" put on it.

So I would like to conclude by reiterating a number of the sentiments that we have heard before and the recommendations, particularly in regard to the special envoy. And I would even like to suggest my institution has offered a suggestion that that position be upgraded to Ambassador level, to raise it in status and show, once again, America's political and moral leadership on this issue, which is needed more now than ever before.

I commend the bipartisan efforts on this. As you heard, we are firmly committed to seeing the fight against anti-Semitism as a bipartisan fight, and I am happy that Members of Congress in both Houses have joined in that very strongly.

I would also like to mention the Anti-Semitism Awareness Act, which is now sitting in Congress, which is an act that attempts to ask the Department of Education to use the working definition of anti-Semitism as a tool to be able to gauge whether anti-Semitism has in fact, happened on college campuses, and it gives us internationally accepted tools to the hands—it puts it in the hands of those people dealing with the issue on U.S. college campuses.

Just two other brief mentions: We have also appealed to the Attorney General for the creation of a task force to deal with the issue of anti-Semitism—the wave of anti-Semitic threats that the American Jewish community is currently facing. And that ties into the other recommendation that I would add, which is the creation of a special portfolio, or the addition of a portfolio that draws together on the domestic front the issue of anti-Semitism as a special envoy to the State Department for foreign affairs. There is no similar focal point in the United States for the issue of anti-Semitism, and we believe that it is time to create that point and, thus, coordinating address—to address the issue of anti-Semitism.

And, finally, I would like to suggest that the Internet service providers as well also adopt both the definition of anti-Semitism, and a working definition of Holocaust denial and distortion as a tool to use in measuring their presence of anti-Semitism and their actions that they can take against it online.

Finally, just to conclude and repeat what I said before, when governments try to legislate history for political purposes, when the Holocaust is taken out of context, is whitewashed, when Holocaust distortion opens the doors for traditional anti-Semitic themes to reenter the governing halls of society, then that is a problem and a challenge and a threat, not only to Jews, but to American democratic values all over.

So I thank the subcommittee for the community to make this statement and for the leadership and activism that you have shown in the past, and I hope to continue cooperating and working together in the future. Thank you.

[The prepared statement of Mr. Weitzman follows:]

TESTIMONY of MARK WEITZMAN
Director of Government Affairs, Simon Wiesenthal Center

Committee on Foreign Affairs
Subcommittee on Africa, Global Health, Global Human Rights and International Organizations

Hearing on "Anti-Semitism Across Borders"

March 22, 2017
Washington D.C.

I want to begin by thanking the Committee, especially Chairman Royce and Ranking Member Engel and Chairman Smith and Ranking Member Bass of the Subcommittee for once again taking the lead in examining the threat currently posed by growing and different manifestations of antisemitism. I am testifying here in my capacity as Director of Government Affairs for the Simon Wiesenthal Center. I am also the Co-Chair of the Committee on Antisemitism and Holocaust Denial of the International Holocaust Remembrance Alliance as well as a board member of the Association of Holocaust Organization, an international umbrella organization of over three hundred organizations and individuals for the advancement of Holocaust education, remembrance and research whose members have also expressed deep concern on these issues.

On June 16, 2004 while waiting for my turn to testify at earlier hearing on antisemitism, held by the Commission on Security and Cooperation in Europe, I heard Natan Sharansky, the famous human rights activist and Israeli leader, describing what was then called the "new antisemitism." As Sharansky defined it "Whereas classical anti-Semitism is aimed at the Jewish people or the Jewish religion, the new antisemitism is aimed at the Jewish State." And, to illustrate the forms this new antisemitism was taking, Sharansky then described the now famous 3 D's of "Double Standards, Demonization and Deligitimization".

Sharansky's formulation built on the insights and experiences of others, such as the late scholar of antisemitism Robert Wistrich who in 1984 identified a "new antisemitic anti-Zionism" in which he described extreme anti-Zionism as the new and only acceptable form which antisemitism could take in a post-Holocaust world. As Wistrich put it "in the post-war Western democracies anti-Zionism has provided a vehicle for the re-emergence of anti-Jewish attitudes which were for some twenty to twenty-five years partially submerged."

These anti-Zionist expressions are not just verbal; frequently inspired by the stream of propaganda that radical Islamists put out online and the financial and political contributions to this campaign that come from some Muslim states and organizations, an increasing number of terrorist have translated words into action and assaulted and murdered Jews throughout Europe and targeted Jewish institutions in Europe and the US. Hatred has moved out from behind the cloak of anti-Zionism and is now nakedly visible as hatred of Jews as an entire generation has been exposed to the most viciously antisemitic propaganda. Having made antisemitism and Holocaust denial core elements of their policy, the repressive regime of Iran stands out as a major source of this propaganda, along with the terrorists of ISIS and Al-Qaeda.

However I think recent events have forced upon us the realization that while much of antisemitism, especially violent and murderous antisemitism, today is indeed filtered through anti-Zionism, a disturbing trend has emerged in which a new form of classical antisemitism itself has reentered the main institutions of civil society in certain areas.

This regeneration of traditional antisemitism is all the more dangerous because, unlike the violent extremists of both left, right and radical Islam, it is now found in government circles and halls of power in countries that we define as Western democracies.

In many ways it is also connected with attempts to distort the history of the Holocaust by whitewashing local collaborators or minimizing or even removing the Jewish identity of the victims. Often this is connected to a political agenda that is concerned with creating a traditionalist national narrative that wants to look back to an idealized past for heroes and models. And since many of these societies have emerged from both Nazi and Communist occupation and oppression, the past that they glorify is frequently the last period of home rule before World War II, and the ideals that they glorify can include versions of the traditional antisemitism that was prevalent before the war.

Perhaps in no country today is the situation more acute than in Poland. There we find senior government officials, such as Minister of Defense Antoni Macierewicz claiming in 2002 that he had read the infamous *Protocols of the Elders of Zion* and that "Experience shows that there are such groups in Jewish circles." He has never publicly retracted that statement, and two other cabinet members, Foreign Minister Witold Waszcykowski and Culture Minister Piotr Glinski have also declined to condemn the *Protocols* when asked to do so.

Macierewicz's original 2002 statement was given to Radio Maryja, the notorious antisemitic radio station that has been condemned by the Vatican for its anti-Jewish remarks. Radio Maryja's history of antisemitism is both well documented and current. Already in 2008 the State Department's *Global Anti-Semitism Report* called Radio Maryja "one of Europe's most blatantly anti-Semitic media venues." More recent examples abound. In September the founder and head of Radio Maryja, Father Tadeusz Rydzyk berated an unruly audience by telling them that they should not be indulging in "synagogue-type behavior".

In November one commentator on the station stated that "the Jewish Lobby in Poland demonstrates its racial solidarity with the Ukrainian oligarchs". In December he made the blatantly antisemitic claim that "The U.S. media and entertainment industry are dependent on the Jewish lobby. It is similar to the Stalinist terror, which was organized and implemented by Jewish communism." And in the same month he made a trip to the US where he spoke in New York, New Jersey and Massachusetts and among other antisemitic remarks referred to the "Jewish faction" which allegedly is ruling Poland.

It is bitterly ironic then that this allegedly Jewish run government has become a huge subsidizer of Radio Maryja. According to news reports the government has paid out the staggering sum of over seven million dollars to Radio Maryja, and was even issuing a postage stamp to commemorate the station's twenty-fifth anniversary.

This is not the only questionable action taken by the current government in Poland. Other recent moves include the covert hiring of an American publicist of Jewish descent to cast antisemitic aspersions at a prominent critic of Poland's current policy. The publicist denied in writing that he was employed by the Polish Ministry of Foreign Affairs, but was fired only when his contract was posted online.

Another was the more recent firing of the Head of the Polish Institute in Berlin, allegedly for "giving too much attention to Jewish subjects". While the Polish Foreign Ministry has denied this was the reason an October memo from the Polish ambassador in Berlin to the director warned "not to overdo the emphasis... on the importance of Polish-Jewish dialogue."

However, the most egregious example so far is the attempt to criminalize Holocaust research and even the memoirs of Holocaust survivors. This is centered on a proposed amendment to Polish law and reads

> "Article 55a. 1. Whoever publicly claims, contrary to the historical facts, the Polish Nation's or the Polish State's responsibility or partial responsibility for the Nazi crimes committed by the German Third Reich ...or for any other crimes against peace, crimes against humanity, or war crimes, or otherwise grossly diminishes the responsibility of the actual perpetrators of these crimes, shall be liable to a fine or imprisonment for up to 3 years...

> Article 55b. Notwithstanding the legal framework applicable in the jurisdiction where the illicit act was committed, this Act shall apply to Polish citizens and to aliens in the event of committing any of the crimes referred to in Articles 55 and 55a".

Thus, according to this law, since Poland was occupied by Nazi Germany during the time of the Holocaust, any person who makes a statement that refers to Polish collaboration or complicity in the murder of the millions of Jews killed on Polish soil is committing a crime. This is not totally a new initiative, as Poland is already trying to move against the eminent Princeton historian Jan Gross. Gross, who previously received the Polish Order of Merit in 1996 is the author of *Neighbors* (Princeton, 2001) which tells of the murder of several hundred Jews in the town of Jedwabne, by their Polish neighbors on July 10, 1941. The book was a National Book Award finalist in 2001 and caused a major controversy in Poland where its findings were hotly debated but did lead two presidents of Poland to apologize for what happened at Jedwabne. In an interview with a German newspaper in 2015 Gross stated that in his opinion Poles murdered more Jews than they killed Germans during the war (a statement that is supported by many leading experts but that is highly controversial in Poland). This led to Gross' being investigated on the charge of libeling the Polish nation (under the law "that any person who publicly insults the Polish nation is punishable by up to three years in prison".) He has since been hauled in for five hours of questioning and the threat continues to hang over him. Indeed, the first prosecutor assigned to his case recommended dropping it, but was overruled by his superior in what appears to be a political decision. But Prof. Gross is not really the focal point here – as an esteemed senior scholar at Princeton he will not suffer from this attempt at censorship of inconvenient history. The full impact of the law can be felt in its chilling effect on less established and younger scholars, who may fear to speak openly on their findings or be dissuaded from even beginning to research the subject of Poland and the Holocaust. This is clearly an attempt to legislate history, and as the renowned Holocaust scholar Prof. Yehuda Bauer with his colleague Prof. Havi Dreifuss wrote "It is not the job of any government (in a democratic country) to determine historical facts, beyond very obvious ones; the fact of the Holocaust, for instance, or the fact of the persecution of Poles by Nazi Germany."

However, there is another aspect of this proposed law that is equally frightening. Should this proposed amendment become law, anyone, anyplace who is convicted of "shaming" Poland's reputation in relation to the Holocaust faces a potential three year prison sentence.

Consider the words of Sigi Isak, born in Berlin and a survivor of the Plaszow labor camp and Gross-Rosen concentration camp who stated "In Poland they were -- they were terrible before the war the Poles. (I) even call them worse than the Germans because they did ugly things in the war."

Or of Abraham Kolski, born in Lodz, Poland and a survivor of the Treblinka death camp who said "I don't say one hundred percent Poles are bad...and maybe a ten percent (of the) Poles are good. The other, even today, very very bad. You can't imagine. You can't imagine. You are an American. You can't imagine. They are worse than the Russians. They are worse then the Germans."

Or of Lonia Mosak, born in Poland and a survivor of Auschwitz who remembered that "we decided we're going back to Poland. ...We didn't realize that Poland was worse than with the Germans. They didn't want any Jew to come there because then they claim their properties. So they didn't want us. So when you went out on the street, you saw laying dead Jews,"

These three statements are available in the archives of the United States Holocaust Memorial Museum. They are far from unique. I have heard similar statements from survivors many times when I was interviewing them for Simon Wiesenthal or for other Nazi war criminal investigations. Their words are the testimony of Holocaust survivors who felt the sting of personal relationships fatally betrayed and who have recounted their emotions and experiences and now, under this proposed new law are potentially facing criminal charges at this late stage of their lives.

In my capacity as Chair of the International Holocaust Remembrance Alliance's (IHRA) Committee on Antisemitism and Holocaust Denial I was asked to participate with three others in a High-Level Mission to Warsaw to discuss the IHRA's great concern over this proposed law. This amendment and the Polish actions clearly fly in the face of the Stockholm Declaration and IHRA's mission, which requires member countries to share a commitment to "to encourage the study of the Holocaust in all its dimensions." And indeed, we would expect Poland, as a member of the IHRA since 1999, to live up to that commitment. However, what I experienced in Warsaw was something different. There I was told directly that the Poles were very upset to see the usage of the term "Polish death camps" still appearing in the West and were determined to try and wipe it out. This was puzzling, because IHRA and most responsible Holocaust related institutions and scholars shared Poland's feeling about the inaccuracy and inappropriateness of that term; indeed I had been instrumental in my own institution removing it from our web site a decade ago. Despite that we were told that since that term still sometimes appeared the Polish government had now decided to legislate what would be legal and what would be illegal in Holocaust discourse, thus creating a new precedent of a Western democratic country potentially criminalizing responsible scholars and Holocaust survivors for their research and memories.

And while Poland might be the most acute example, it is far from the only one. In Hungary, over the past few years, there were a series of government inspired initiatives that also attempted to distort the history of the Holocaust to favor a narrow political agenda. They began with the insertion into the Preamble of the new constitution a clause that exempted Hungary from any responsibility for actions that occurred under Nazi (and Communist) occupation; this appearing to absolve Hungary of any collaboration in the deportation and murder of almost four hundred and fifty thousand Jews after the Nazi occupation in 1944. However, the reality is that the Nazi unit that organized and supervised the occupation never numbered more than one hundred twenty five men and could not have successfully accomplished its mission without local collaboration, or that the mass murder of Budapest's remaining Jewish population took place after the Nazis pulled out and the city was ruled by the local Arrow Cross collaborators.

Other actions included the insertion into the national curriculum of antisemitic writers, or the erection of statues to politicians who were notorious for their antisemitism. One of them, Balint Homan even introduced the Hungarian version of the infamous Nuremberg laws which began the disenfranchisement of Hungarian Jews and opened up the door to their despoiling and eventual deportation. Another flash point was the proposed Holocaust museum that was to be under the direction of an ideologue whose writings contained antisemitic themes and who refused to be open about her proposed plan for the museum. All this led to a crisis in which Mazsihisz, the official Jewish community organization, felt compelled to boycott all of the government sponsored commemorations of the 70th anniversary of the 1944 Hungarian deportations. Through my role at IHRA I was deeply involved in these efforts, and I would like to especially thank Chairman Smith who wrote a pivotal letter to Prime Minister Orban that I believe helped the Prime Minister understand the damage that these efforts were causing to Hungary's reputation. The efforts of Ira Forman, then our Special Envoy on Antisemitism were also extremely helpful, and the vigorous and bipartisan response here and the reaction internationally apparently helped convince the Prime Minister to reassess the government's position and to finally announce that the museum director would be pulled off the project which would only be finished with the cooperation of the Jewish community and international experts, and no more government funcing or land would be made available for the construction of monuments to questionable World War II era figures.

We can see a similar pattern in Croatia where the local Jewish community has felt it necessary to also boycott official government Holocaust Remembrance Commemorations for the past two years. The first time it was connected to what the community claimed was the "revitalizing" of the Ustasha, the brutal Croatian collaborationist movement. An example of this was the appointment of Zlatko Hasanbegovic as the Minister of Culture. Hasanbegovic had been photographed wearing the cap and insignia of the Ustashe, and had published articles earlier defending the Ustashe. While he was the Minister of Culture he screened a film at the Jasenovac concentration camp that claimed that the number of victims killed in the camp was less than half than historians had been estimating (taking the generally recognized total of close to eighty to one hundred thousand and cutting it to between twenty to forty thousand victims) thus encouraging those who would minimize the Ustashe crimes and claim that the camp was actually only a labor camp.

Hasanbagovic only lasted a few months in office, but even after his departure problems persist. This year the community reacted to the erection of a plaque with Ustashe slogans in front of the camp. In the words of Jewish community leader Ognjen Kraus "We took the decision on the basis of reactions by the government, parliament and the president. The problem is not (just) a plaque in Jasenovac including the Ustasha salute, but the relativisation of everything (to do with the Holocaust." This includes a judge who in a case involving a threat to the director of the camp also questioned the number of victims, and school officials who this past January removed an exhibit about Anne Frank because they considered it unfair to the Ustashe. And finally the president of Croatia was photographed holding the Ustashe flag last November. To be fair, the President has also condemned the Ustashe, the school officials were reprimanded, and as mentioned above Hasanbegovic is no longer a minister. Nevertheless, the atmosphere still remains toxic enough for the community to have taken the drastic step of boycotting this past January's Holocaust commemoration and for civil society to address an open letter to the Croatian political leadership calling it to develop a culture of remembrance that would allow Croatia to accurately portray and learn from its past.

In Serbia a few weeks ago proposed new legislation that would create a state commission to commemorate Holocaust victims was leaked and immediately criticized by the local Jewish community and human rights activists for not mentioning the role of Serbian collaborators during the war. Although officials have cautioned that this proposal was not in final form it comes on the heels of an ongoing effort by Serbian apologists to rehabilitate Milan Nedic, the Prime minister of Serbia's collaborationist government during World War II. Under his rule Belgrade was the first European city to be declared *Judenfrei* (free of Jews) and ninety percent of Serbia's Jews were murdered.

Ukraine is another example of a country attempting to legislate history, especially the history of World War II. In an attempt to whitewash local Nazi collaborators and antisemites it recently passed a law called Law No. 2538-, "On the legal status and honoring of fighters for Ukraine's independence in the 20th century." This law states that "the public denial of...the just cause of the fighters for Ukrainian independence in the 20th century insults the dignity of the Ukrainian people and is illegal." However, these "independence fighters" were in actuality members of organizations (OUN, UPA) who deeply cooperated with the Nazis and are considered responsible by historians for murdering about one hundred thousand Poles and tens of thousands of Jews based on the crudest antisemitism.

Ironically, the other country that is also attempting to censor history is Vladimir Putin's Russia. Russia has successfully applied a law that forbids the publication of what they describe as "falsehoods" about the Soviet Union's role during World War II. In one case a journalist was convicted after writing the incontrovertible historical fact that "the Communists and Germany jointly invaded Poland, sparking off World War II. That is, communism and Nazism closely collaborated ..." Although the entire world is aware of the Ribbentrop-Molotov pact of 1939 and the joint Nazi-Soviet invasion of Poland in September 1939, Putin's Russia has now made it a crime to speak or write about it.

This attempts cannot be described as Holocaust denial. Today to be uncloaked and exposed as an active denier means the end of one's respectability as David Irving, the Holocaust denying and antisemitic British writer found out in 2000. Irving sued the American historian Deborah Lipstadt and her publisher for libel and lost; as a result of the verdict in the trial Irving went from a writer whose work was cited by major historians to an isolated and ignored figure reduced to peddling guided tours to small groups of sympathizers and speaking at neo-Nazi conventions.

However, distortion of the Holocaust is a different matter entirely. Here we are not speaking of outright denial, the kind that still lingers in disreputable corners and as the official policy of the Iranian government, but rather the position that pays lip service to the reality of the Holocaust but tries to evade assigning responsibility for political reasons. This type of Holocaust distortion has been around ever since the end of the war. A version of it was official policy in many Communist countries, where while the number of victims was sometimes even exaggerated; the specific Jewish component of the identity of the victims and the focus of Nazi policy was erased in a politically motivated rendering of all the victims as generic victims of fascism, perhaps most famously in the original plaque at Babi Yar in Kyiv.

These attempts to craft and apply laws to evade and distort the reality of the Holocaust in an attempt to strengthen national myths were a major reason that the 31 member states of the International Holocaust Remembrance Alliance felt the need to adopt by consensus a "Working Definition of Holocaust Denial and Distortion" in 2013.
(https://www.holocaustremembrance.com/working-definition-holocaust-denial-and-distortion)
As the primary author of that definition I was determined that the inclusion of the section on distortion was vital to the definition's integrity. Without it any definition would be limited and would avoid the most pressing current issue. There were some countries that preferred to leave out the aspect of distortion precisely because it allowed them to continue to politicize the Holocaust. However, because of our (the combined experts and diplomats) refusal to accept any watered down version it took five years of negotiations before we could get the Working Definition adopted. But having successfully achieved adoption of the definition, the international community now has a benchmark that includes and describes this current version of Holocaust distortion and can be used to challenge those misleading narratives.

In this climate of high level distortion of the Holocaust it should be no surprise that according to a report by Israel's ambassador to Sweden since last spring lectures and school appearances by Holocaust survivors have disrupted by a small skinhead group called the Nordic Resistance Movement and the police have refused to provide security for the schools under the grounds that the skinheads "do not yet appear to provoke violence."!

Sad to say, the United States is not exempt from some of these issues as well. Just last week a synagogue in Seattle was vandalized and on it was spray painted "The Holocaust is fake history". This explains the consternation and strong reactions of so many segments of the Jewish community in the United States when this past January 27 the White House statement on Holocaust Remembrance Day omitted any mention of Jews. The US has long been the leader in maintaining the need for historical integrity on this subject, and especially in light of the disturbing trends noted above, our leadership is needed more than ever.

Alongside this disturbing international trend is the rise in anti-Semitism on college campuses here at home. In the first six months of 2016, there was a 45% increase in anti-Semitic activity on college campuses. What should be safe academic spaces are quickly becoming hotbeds of anti-Jewish bias, with students each year reporting greater discomfort at publicly identifying as Jewish or as supporters of Israel.

Last term, the Senate passed by unanimous consent a bill that is critical to combatting rising anti-Semitism on US college campuses. The Anti-Semitism Awareness Act would require the Department of Education "to take into consideration the definition of anti-Semitism as part of [its] assessment of whether the alleged practice was motivated by anti-Semitic bias." This definition would serve as an essential tool in interpreting whether harassment, intimidation, or other seemingly discriminatory behavior directed at Jewish students is motivated by anti-Semitism and should be investigated. The definition is a global standard, which is adopted by the State Department and the 31 governments that are members of the International Holocaust Remembrance Alliance. The Anti-Semitism Awareness Act is the best tool for pushing back against anti-Semitism on college campuses while protecting free speech, explicitly stating that "Nothing in this Act, or an amendment made by this Act, shall be construed to diminish or infringe upon any right protected under the First Amendment of the Constitution of the United States."

While the Simon Wiesenthal Center is firmly committed to the First Amendment and as shown above rejects government attempts to censor historical and political dialogue, we recognize the need for encouraging service providers to deal with the flood of hate speech, threats, attempts to intimidate, stereotypes, wild conspiracies and calls to violence emanating from both right and left wing extremist groups and individuals. With the power of social media comes the need for a sense of responsibility, and we call upon the service providers to live up to their terms of service and to begin to consistently and firmly reject those postings that qualify as antisemitic in particular and hate speech in general. Specifically, we strongly urge that the companies immediately adopt the two internationally accepted definitions of Holocaust Denial and Distortion and of Antisemitism that have been adopted by the 31 nations of the International Holocaust Remembrance Alliance. These working definitions were specifically adopted with the aim of providing a tool for exactly this purpose; that is to give those who are wrestling with these issues a tool that was crafted by international experts and adopted by political representatives of those 31 countries with the aim of providing a common language and understanding of both antisemitism and Holocaust denial and distortion for practical use.

With all the difficult situations that have been noted above I would like to close with some positive examples drawn from our direct experience.

As noted above, thanks to the combined efforts of committed international experts, diplomats and the local Jewish community, it appears that efforts to distort the history of the Holocaust in Hungary have been halted, at least temporarily. This shows what can be accomplished by people committed to maintaining the integrity of the historical narrative of the Holocaust and sets a powerful example for us to follow.

The adoption by the 31 member nations of the IHRA of the two "Working Definitions" represents an extremely significant international effort to fight antisemitism in its different manifestations. Here I would like to specifically acknowledge the vital contribution of the Past Chair of the IHRA, Amb. Mihnea Constantinescu of Romania, who was responsible for politically shepherding the antisemitism definition through to its successful adoption. Having been responsible for introducing this definition in IHRA and working closely with Amb. Constantinescu allowed me to see his total commitment to the definition's adoption. I am glad to also recognize the efforts of my colleague in the US IHRA delegation, Dr. Robert Williams, the incoming Chair of IHRA's Committee on Antisemitism and Holocaust Denial, for his efforts in working toward the adoption of the definition. And I want to also thank the Special Envoy on Holocaust Issues, Thomas Yazdgerdi, and the Deputy Director of that office, Liz Nakian, for their strong leadership of the US IHRA delegation.

I would also like to point to the success of a country, Azaerbaijan that is 96% Muslim and that is known as a country that protects religious freedom. There are some significant domestic issues, but the Jewish community is at home there. On Sept. 29 the Simon Wiesenthal Center opened its renowned exhibit *"People, Book, Land: The 3,500 Year Relationship of the Jewish People with the Holy Land"* in Baku. This is the same exhibit that Chairman Royce and Ranking Member Engel sponsored in Congress two years ago, and I want to publicly acknowledge and thank them for their leadership.

Another country, Bahrain, was just visited by a delegation from the Simon Wiesenthal Center for meetings that included the King of Bahrain. While there our delegation saw Shia and Suni mosques together, just one half block from a church and Christian compound. And, during the recent Hindu holiday of *Maha Shivratri*, over ten thousand Hindu's came for the festival. Although not directly referring to antisemitism, this example is significant in that it shows what is possible in our world.

I would like to conclude with a series of recommendations.

First is the appointment of a strong Special Envoy on Antisemitism with sufficient funding, staffing and political support for effective action. The previous Special Envoy, Ira Forman, built on the accomplishments of his predecessors Gregg Rickman and Hannah Rosenthal, and became a vigorous and forceful advocate in fighting international antisemitism. Fighting antisemitism has always been a bipartisan commitment, and in today's fractured political world it is more necessary than ever that the US maintain its diplomatic and moral leadership in this issue. Indeed, we would strongly suggest that the position even be upgraded, to that of Ambassador, thus demonstrating the importance attached by our government to this issue.
Currently seven other countries have followed the US in creating such a position, and the European Union has also appointed a representative on the issue. It would send a terrible signal now for the US to appear to be backing away from the issue just as others are beginning to engage on it.

Second is continuing to push for the adoption of the IHRA's Working Definition of Antisemitism.
The definition has been adopted by the United Kingdom, the city of London and Israel. Other countries are considering its adoption as well. Thanks to the efforts of Rabbi Baker it was almost adopted by the OSCE, obtaining the backing of fifty six of the OSCE members, with only Russia blocking it. We would like to return to the OSCE and try again, but it requires strong US backing to have any chance to succeed.

Third would be the adoption in the US of the Anti-Semitism Awareness Act, which is based on the IHRA definition. Adoption would offer an expert derived internationally accepted yardstick to define antisemitism on our campuses and would provide necessary clarity and protection to students, administrators and everyone associated with college life.

Fourth would be the creation of a special Task Force by the Attorney General to deal with the ongoing series of threats to the Jewish community in the US. These unprecedented threats have challenged basic assumptions about security and belonging for American Jews. The immediate establishment of such a Task Force would provide a strong symbol to all that there can be no place for antisemitism in American life.

Fifth would be the designation of a specific government office to function as a central focal point for domestic issues relating to antisemitism. Currently the responsibilities are split between a variety of agencies and departments, such as the Department of Education, the   FBI, Homeland Security, etc. The designation of such an office would provide coordination and an address for both the Jewish community and for those working on the issue.

Sixth, both in Europe and in the US, it is essential that security services to protect the Jewish communities of those countries continue to be provided by the home countries. Security for residents is a basic human right and expectation, and the Jewish communities should not be charged extra for the right to live in a safe environment. Both the political level, judiciary and law enforcement need to take the threats against these communities seriously and to respond vigorously and in timely fashion to threats and actions that imperil the safety of Jews and Jewish institutions.

Finally, as mentioned above, internet service providers need to recognize that they share in the common responsibility for the state of our societies. As with other industries, the drive for profits carries responsibilities as well. Thus we urge that they immediately adopt the IHRA Working Definitions of Antisemitism and Holocaust Denial and Distortion to serve as tools to measure whether specific posts are in violation of the terms of service that already exist. This is a simple first step toward solving a problem that they have helped to create by turning a blind eye to the content displayed, particularly on social media and sometimes to the ensuing results as well.

Thank you very much for your leadership, commitment and action in fighting antisemitism.

———————

Mr. SMITH. Mr. Weitzman, thank you for your extraordinarily effective leadership and your recommendations and your analysis of the state of affairs as of today and looking forward.

Let me just ask you if that report that will be released in about a week, is that something we might be able to include in our record? Because we will leave the record open if you——

Mr. WEITZMAN. We usually—it usually comes out in electronic form. I could see if we have a version that we could include. We will try to do that.

Mr. SMITH. If you would, that could be helpful, I think, for the record, and for all of us to read and digest.

Mr. WEITZMAN. Absolutely. Thank you.

Mr. SMITH. The Ambassador-at-Large, that is something that we are looking at, legislative text right now, so we will get back to you on how we are proceeding on that.

In November 2015, I authored H. Res. 354, and it passed 418-0 on the House floor. Many of you helped us with the text, with the analysis of what ought to be in there, and I deeply appreciate the insights you provided. And we did call, in the operative part of the resolution, urging the United States Government to work closely with the European governments and their law enforcement agencies to "formally recognize, partner, train, and share information with Jewish community security groups to strengthen preparedness, prevention, mitigation and response related to anti-Semitic attacks and to support related research initiatives." There are many operative clauses, but that was the first.

And I am wondering if, in your view, that happened. Do you believe it is going to happen, you know, hopefully in an expanded way, or, at least, consistent with this request of the administration, because it is an ongoing request? And Rabbi Baker, if you might—others, if you would like as well—maybe share with us what you think are best practices. We need to share every best practice we have, but what can we learn from the UK, from France, and others, particularly the United Kingdom, which I agree with you have done much—they have so many challenges, particularly in London. You and I were there at the House of Commons when we both spoke to a large group, of lawmakers from around the world, and it was very clear that the United Kingdom was really trying to step up to the plate on these horrific crimes. Are there things we might learn from them?

But, again, this was passed in 2015, so there were—and Ira Forman probably could provide us some information on this as well—how well that was implemented, because it was bipartisan, 418-0, and your thoughts going forward with the new administration to make sure that there are no gaps?

Rabbi BAKER. Well, we could——

Mr. SMITH. Paul, if you want to start, then we will go right down the line.

Mr. GOLDENBERG. So I think I will address the police aspect of it, which is——

Mr. SMITH. Thank you.

Mr. GOLDENBERG [continuing]. Where I am very engaged and involved abroad right now.

We are working on the ground in Belgium with the Belgian police. We are actually working on the ground in Molenbeek. You have an area called Soblan, which is a very heavily Jewish area, and, of course, you have Molenbeek, which is an area that the majority of the population is Muslim. And we are working on the ground there with the police building—it is called BCOT, building communities of trust between these communities, this is through the Rutgers project, in particular, a colleague of yours, Chairman Smith, Congressman Smith, which is John Farmer, former Attorney General of New Jersey.

So it is engaging the communities, the security groups, and the police. It has been a bit of a challenge, but I will tell you, I think there has been tremendous progress over the past 24 months. It is really about compelling the national police agencies, or the local police agencies, to share information with the Jewish communities, really demystifying the process. That is extremely integral to better communications between the two.

The Jewish communities need information. They need information that will allow them to be safer, and the law enforcement agencies also need to work much more collaboratively with those Jewish security agencies not only for the sharing of information, but joint training, joint exercises, et cetera, because it is really a quid pro quo: Information comes up, and information comes down. So it is really creating a clear pathway of communication between the national and local police agencies and the Jewish communities that are sworn to protect them.

We have a much more mature relationship here. The American Jewish community, through the works of SCN, Security Community Network, ADL, and other organizations, it has been a very mature relationship. These relationships have been for decades, I know. And there are some really remarkable best practices here that, for years, have been shared with our colleagues abroad.

At the end of the day, these communities have to rely on their local police, and that is where it starts, and that is where, unfortunately, it——

Mr. SMITH. Could I ask you, as to Stacy Burdett's point about local police here and in Europe? Is it getting down to that level so that the local law enforcement—I mean, we put that into our resolution as well, ensure law enforcement personnel are effectively trained to monitor, prevent, and respond to anti-Semitic violence, and partner with Jewish communities. And that second part, partner with Jewish communities, is so extremely important so that there is that dialogue, so if there is something that is happening, or there is a threat, there is a response that is informed by law enforcement.

Mr. GOLDENBERG. Is that here in the United States or abroad?

Mr. SMITH. Here and abroad.

Mr. GOLDENBERG. If I will tell you, here in the United States, absolutely. The relationships between State, local, and Federal law enforcement are absolutely extraordinary. And I know—I am not going to speak for the Anti-Defamation League, but our two organizations are in constant contact every day with our State, local, and Federal law enforcement agencies. They not only have been sharing information as best they can with regard to active investigations, but I will tell you during this situation where we see nearly 170 bomb threats against Jewish centers, that the U.S. Department of Homeland Security deployed nearly 120 professionals. Every State in the country has what is called a protective security advisor. These are very high-level experienced individuals that were literally deployed to work and engage with the Jewish community centers not just for partnership purposes, but to provide real, viable expertise to them. So that is how far it went.

And we met with the FBI just recently, 2 weeks ago, with Director Comey. And, undoubtedly, every Jewish leader that walked out of there had an extremely high level of confidence in the Bureau, what they are doing, and how engaged they are.

Mr. SMITH. If I could just walk right down.

Rabbi BAKER. So let me outline where I think we have succeeded and where your legislation clearly resonates, and where there are still challenges, at least in Europe.

One of the significant challenges has been to, essentially, get those European Jewish communities themselves to engage, to develop the kind of professionalism to know how to handle security issues, and that varies greatly community by community. As we mentioned, the UK and France are very good models. Other countries are coming to this late. But there are efforts, really, to get all of them up to a certain level.

At that point, the concern is also the kind of relationships that can develop with local and national authorities; police, intelligence gathering agencies, and the like.

That also varies greatly from place to place. That is one of the sad realities, and we have tried to leverage good practices in one country to encourage, to push other countries to follow suit.

As you may recall, in my OSCE role, I made an official visit to Copenhagen, which happen to have been 5 months before that terrorist attack that left one security volunteer dead. Authorities in Denmark said to me, we have a "relaxed approach" to security. A "relaxed approach." And by that, they meant, they were concerned, that their citizens would feel uncomfortable if they saw armed police in front of buildings. And so for that reason, they weren't providing police in front of the synagogue or the school with, ultimately, the tragic results that took place.

There was a mindset that had to be addressed, and ultimately changed. And in dealing with this issue of security, if the governments don't recognize the genuine threat, it is hard to feel you are going to succeed.

Those terrible incidents maybe have helped galvanized that attention. But it still has challenges in finding its way into the different communities and municipalities.

We mentioned the challenges in Malmo, Sweden. When I was there this past September, and I asked the person responsible in the municipality for security, about there really not being any give-and-take communication with the local Jewish community, he said to me—and he is a veteran himself of police—I don't get responses from Stockholm, from the national government, when they know we have threats in this community.

So part of the problem isn't just the communication between Jewish community professionals and government, it is even within governments themselves that leave groups, leave people vulnerable. So this has been part of these issues, clearly, where you can, and some of these best practice models, point to good cooperation, sharing of information, not only of threats, but of collecting data and the like. Because, often, Jewish communities with professional monitoring agencies will find that community members, who have experienced incidents, will report to them even if they are reluctant to report to police. They know they are going to be taken seriously. And a good relationship means that same information can then find its way to government authorities.

So those are some of the examples where, again, we have had progress, but still challenges remain.

Mr. SMITH. Go ahead, Stacy.

Ms. BURDETT. I just want to suggest three ideas on this topic: You asked about local law enforcement. We are in a period of transition. We haven't heard an affirmation of the Department of Justice's commitment to train law enforcement on data collection, reporting, hate crime investigations, prosecutorial skills that they need. That is something that is very high on our wish list as we look at these bomb threats and the rise in hate crimes in the country.

So every day is a good day to reaffirm. If you want to see the best hate crime training manual that I have seen, the FBI has one, and we should use it. It is very good. It includes scenarios that all kinds of NGOs have worked on.

And speaking of training manuals, I know, Mr. Chairman, it can be important when a Member of Congress inquires into a government program. You know quite well the international law enforcement academies that our FBI runs on every continent, and the ILEA has a hate crime curriculum that they are using. It is a training that has been delivered. It is a propriety document, and it might be something that you might want to request from the State Department INL, to take a look at that curriculum and how it is being used and how is that existing training on hate crime, how we can make sure that it is also helping law enforcement officers get the skills to address anti-Semitism. So that is just our own training that we are already doing.

And we also have an existing interagency initiative that has been, for a while, coordinated out of the White House that brings together law enforcement agencies to make sure there is a coordinated and vigorous effort to investigate hate crimes and reach out to communities. So those are three very concrete things that I think would be useful if it were requested by Members of Congress. Thank you.

Mr. WEITZMAN. I just would like to add two very brief points. One is that my colleagues are continuing their training sessions on digital terrorism and hate with law enforcement on a basic local level. We just had a session in Chicago about 2 weeks ago. But I also point out one area of concern, which Rabbi Baker can certainly address as well very deeply, that we hear periodically through some of the European countries that they no longer want to bear the costs of paying for security, and they would like to pass that on to the local Jewish community. I find that very troubling, and I think it is something that we need to reemphasize the point that security is something that needs to be provided to all citizens without their having to pay extra for the right to live and exist in those countries.

Mr. SMITH. Just a few final questions, then I will yield to my good friend from New York.

In one of my previous hearings that I have had, as I indicated quite a few, about 18 or 19 on combating anti-Semitism, and every time we learn things that just jump off the page as—didn't know it was that bad here or there, or that this particular practice was emerging as a more common and prevalent practice.

One of them, in February 2013, I chaired a hearing on "Anti-Semitism, A Growing Threat To All Faiths," and we tried to bring in how Catholics, Muslims, and others need to speak out more robustly against anti-Semitism. But we did have one individual, Willy Silberstein, from the Swedish Committee Against Anti-Semitism, testify, and I had a number of press people who came afterwards and said, Sweden? It is that bad in Sweden? And he said— and you mentioned it, Rabbi Baker, in your comments orally about Sweden, briefly, but he said, Let me start by telling you about Shneur Kesselman. He is a rabbi born in the United States. He is working in the Swedish city of Malmo, which is rather infamous for its anti-Semitism in recent years. What differs him from other Jews of Malmo is that people can see that he is Jewish. He wears traditional clothes.

For some years now, he has been systematically harassed. People spit on him, throw cans after him, threaten him, and call him things like a bloody Jew. He points out in his testimony that there is a large group of Muslims there. He does make the point that a large portion of the Muslim immigrants in Sweden are not anti-Semitic, but also that there are some that are. And that seems to be the game changer in that particular nation.

And I am wondering, if they can't get it right in Sweden, which is known for its nonviolence and very tolerant attitudes, it is not a good sign, in my opinion. So I wonder if you might speak to that, Rabbi, what you found most recently in Sweden. Has it gotten any better?

I remember at the Berlin Conference, the chief rabbi of Berlin and I had dinner together, and he said it is not what it looks like here. He said, If I travel with traditional garb, and I get onto a tram or a bus, I take—or feel and will—it is not just something he senses. He will have comments made. And he said, this is in Berlin in 2004. And he said, you know, so many Jewish individuals go out of their way to de-emphasize their Jewish character and—by not wearing traditional garb, as this particular man in Sweden did. So that was a take-away from me with the chief rabbi in Berlin.

Let me also say, Rabbi, if you could maybe speak to this, as you might know, as you all know—you know it for certain, because you helped us write it, and gave insight—the International Religious Freedom Act bill, the Frank Wolf bill that I am the prime author of, it took years to get enacted, it was signed in late December, has a number of strong, mutually enforcing provisions to it. And I think it will make a difference. It requires far more robust training than our State Department officers, DCMs and departing Ambassadors are getting as of now. They have not gotten it.

The dream of 1998, when the IRFA bill was passed, Frank Wolf's bill, was that, okay. They have left that out. It is about time that combating anti-Semitism and all of the other religious freedom issues were really included in that training, and it turned out to be far less than what any of us thought the implementation phase would include. We now have good, strong language that makes it much stronger. And, again, Ira worked on that, as you pointed out in your number six recommendation. So we have to make sure to monitor that and that it is being done well.

But we also put in a provision, Rabbi, and you referenced this in your oral remarks, about the persecution of lawyers, politicians, or other human rights advocates seeking to defend rights of members of religious groups or highlight religious freedom violations, prohibitions on ritual animal slaughter or male infant circumcision, to include that in the annual IRFA reports. So that will be in this report. It is required by this legislation. It was signed into law in the middle of December. So we are going to make sure that that is in there.

Because, you know, as Sharansky said in Berlin, you can't fight something if you don't chronicle it. So we have to get the chronicalling going in this aspect as well. So you might want to speak to Sweden and to this provision.

Rabbi BAKER. Sure. With regard to Sweden—and I did, actually, also see Willy Silberstein when I was there this past September, and as I noted before, I was in Malmo.

Actually, for the first time, they did apprehend and prosecute a perpetrator of an attack on this rabbi in Malmo. I guess that is good news. And I think we have been able—they have been able to find him in an apartment closer to the synagogue, so at least he is not this sort of visible target that he had become.

The fact is that the challenge goes much beyond just this single rabbi.

Malmo has really been the entry point for refugees and migrants coming into Sweden. And as I mentioned earlier, many of them come with attitudes from their host countries, anti-Jewish, anti-Semitic, anti-Western in various ways. In 2013, there were 800 foreigners that the city had to deal with.

In 2015, they had 13,000. So the challenges are really dramatic, and they are not necessarily up to it. I think we recognize that.

One bit of, I want to say, positive news—and this also concerns Malmo—are efforts to secure a rabbi that will come to the city with a specific focus of working on interreligious and, in particular, Jewish-Muslim activities. And in this case, the Swedish Government would fund this project. At the time I was there, they were trying to identify someone. I don't know whether it has yet been implemented, but I think that was a good effort to say, let's see what we can do. Because we know, as I have said earlier, much of this difficulty goes with attitudes in the Muslim community. And this would be a program focused, really, explicitly on that.

I am very happy to know that in the International Religious Freedom Report this issue will be identified. We have been pushing, also, within the OSCE and hope and expect that there will be a conference later this year, probably in July, that will focus on religious freedom and ritual practice to try to bring together those forces that are making efforts to push back on these restrictions and, again, to say, this is an essential element of freedom of religion and religious practice.

I think, as we have seen before—when we have a U.S. report on interreligious freedom, on human rights, on anti-Semitism, it gets attention. Our respective organizations may do something similar. We will put out our reports, but in reality, governments truly pay attention if the U.S. Government is citing this.

So thank you so much for being able to see that this happens.

Mr. SMITH. Mr. Suozzi.

Mr. SUOZZI. Mr. Chairman, let me say, again, that I want to thank you for your leadership on these issues. And I want you to know this is a very important issue to me, combating anti-Semitism, and human rights in general. And I will always try and serve as a partner to you in any efforts you have in this regard.

I want to thank the witnesses for their fantastic work that they have done with their careers and throughout their lives on these issues. And I want to welcome them here today. To make you feel welcome, I want to say bruchim habaim, and welcome you here to Washington today and thank you for the work that you are doing. Again, I am a former mayor and county executive and very comfortable with the issues you are talking about regarding law enforcement, having overseen very large police departments as Nassau County executive, and a smaller police department as Glen Cove mayor and know how important local law enforcement, both here in America and abroad, and the training that they receive on these issues is so essential. So, anything the chairman wants to try and promote in that respect, I will be happy to support him in those efforts.

It is important we say on the record that Jews have been persecuted for centuries, as all of you know, but it is important that I say it as well. And that, you know, this is a persecuted minority. There are over 2 billion Christians in the world. There are 1½ billion Muslims in the world. There are 900 million Hindus in the world. There are 376 million Buddhists in the world. There are 23 million Sikhs in the world, and there are only 14 to 15 million Jews. And when you think about the number of 6 million people annihilated during the Holocaust, what an incredible statistic that is. And the persecution that the Jews have suffered for centuries is something we have to start worrying about again today.

We need to look at what is happening in the world right now. There are other minority groups that are being discriminated against, and there is something that is happening related to the Internet, something that is happening related to our political dialogue and the way that people treat each other generally in high public places, in the way that they talk to each other with a lack of civility, where it has become almost acceptable to demean people and to treat people with less than their human dignity.

And I wanted to ask each of you to just tell me what you think is happening in the world today that we are seeing these rises happen? What are the factors that are contributing to this uptick in hate crimes, certainly, for Jews, certainly, but throughout our societies throughout the world today. What is happening? Is it the Internet? Is it people that were underground before, it is easier for them to express themselves utilizing social media? Is it because of leadership in the world? Is it because people feel threatened because of their economic circumstances? What is it that is happening in the world today that we see this uptick in anti-Semitism and other discrimination?

Mr. Goldenberg?

Mr. GOLDENBERG. Well, one of the things—and my distinguished colleagues could probably really elaborate more so on what I am going to say, but I am not looking to simplify it, but I had the honor of working closely with you when you were county executive, I am very aware of the good works you did out in the county on bias crimes and hate crimes——

Mr. SUOZZI. Thank you.

Mr. GOLDENBERG [continuing]. Working with the police department.

And as someone that, actually, was responsible for the prosecution and investigation of these crimes in the State of New Jersey for the Attorney General's office, I am speaking, again, through a different set of optics. Back in the day when we were investigating these types of crimes, and we had leaflets, calling for death to the Jews or Jews to the ovens, which are extremely heinous in itself, those words were leafletted on maybe 100 cars. And those that were distributing the leaflets would get tired and go back to their basements and go back to their disheveled printers. And I am not making light of this, by no means.

Today, Congressman, with a single click of a finger, you can reach tens of thousands, if not hundreds of thousands, some of which are now much more emboldened. They feed off of each other.

You know, but the old cliche, some say, well, the Internet, First Amendment, sticks and stones will break your bones, but there are statistics to show that dozens and dozens and dozens of individuals who have been involved, or engaged, or have perpetrated murders tied to extremist views, have done so because they were inspired through the Internet. Stormfront, one of the most vial, vial Internet sites out there, Breivik in Norway, who killed dozens of children; Miller, who shot three wonderful human beings out in Kansas City; and our latest individual that just was found guilty for shooting nine wonderful souls down, taking out nine wonderful souls in Charleston, South Carolina. The common denominator between them is they visited the same site. They visited the same site.

So it is the old cliche, it is the best of times and the worst of times, because we have this wonderful tool. But, again, my colleagues can elaborate much more.

Mr. SUOZZI. That is the point Tom Friedman makes in his most recent book, "Thank You for Being Late," is that, you know, the Internet makes this opportunity for makers to do great things and for breakers, the people that want to try to take us down.

Rabbi BAKER. Well, you ask a real challenging question, because there is an uptick. And the why is really one, I think, we all wrestle with.

It reminded me of something that goes back now, I think, almost 25 years. AJC, at the time, was doing attitude surveys in different European countries. We would ask how people felt about Jews as neighbors and so on, but about other minority groups too, to really try to get a more comprehensive picture not only of anti-Semitism, but of other prejudices. We were presenting one of these surveys done in Germany at a press conference in Berlin. There was a pretty significant degree of anti-Jewish feeling, but also anti other-group sentiments, I want to say, maybe, ranging from maybe 20 percent up to, maybe, 80 percent in terms of the degree of negativity depending on the group.

And someone asked about such surveys at the time in the United States, and there have been. And what was interesting was the range of negative attitudes. The range itself was much lower. Maybe beginning at 5 or 6 percent, and going up, in the worst case, to 20-plus percent depending on the group.

One of the Germans in this press conference said, as a way of explaining the more negative responses there, maybe people here are just more willing to speak their mind, to tell you what they really feel and that, perhaps, those surveys done in America, people were inhibited; they didn't want to say what they really felt. And it seemed like an answer, although at the time my colleague said, well, you know, maybe that is true. But the first step, at the very least, is to make saying those things taboo. Even if you think it, you shouldn't feel free to say it.

And, so, it has always struck me, this is a basic lesson. It goes whether it is the old way of communicating in broad sides, or just in public speeches, or in the new means we have today, but it comes back to the same thing: We need to, as a first step, at least, make sure these kinds of racist, xenophobic, anti-Semitic expressions, aren't acceptable. And we all have a role in doing that.

Mr. STOZZI. That is an excellent point, Rabbi. Thank you.

Mr. WEITZMAN. I agree with what both my distinguished colleagues have said before, and I would say that just to make it very graphic, when I—one of the first articles I wrote about extremism on the Internet was for a conference at Oxford, I think, in the year 2000. And I entitled it, "The Internet is More Powerful Than a Sword." And that was, actually, the message at that point that was taken from the writings of the neo-Nazi online. They, themselves, saw it as more powerful. Actually, if we begin, and want a good understanding of this, Stormfront, which Paul mentioned, is basically credited with being the original neo-Nazi site online from 1995. Actually, the reality is already in the mid-1980s, in the old dial-up BBS systems, we found a neo-Nazi site from West Virginia, for example, was one of the first online. And it became the prototype. It had a library of neo-Nazi writings, it had a list of race traders, things of that effect on it, point systems where people were already targeted, ranging from leaders of civil rights organizations, Federal judges, Jewish leaders, et cetera, and it was already established by the turn of the millennia.

So this that has been prevalent ever since the technology began. And it teaches us, it is not the technology; it is the human beings involved with it. So what my colleague said I agree wholeheartedly, I think that the sense of responsibility is something that is lacking. And I would also add that I think one of the things that we allow— and you made the point of political language becoming de-based and very highly charged. And Chairman Smith has referred to Natan Sharansky's remarks a couple of times already. I think

58

what he was pointing out and talking about was how the criticism to Israel became hostility to Israel. Israel became identified and accepted as identification in certain elite circles, media circles, and so on, identified with Nazi acts, with an apartheid state, with genocide, with concentration camps, and this was then extended to the totality of the Jewish people.

The effects of the Holocaust were turned around, were inverted, where the victims became the perpetrators. So we have a system, or a culture, where, in certain ways, very highly emotionally charged language was used to create not just disagreement, but hate, and stereotypes were built into it. The opposition that Rabbi Baker mentioned to some of the traditional acts of Jewish religious practice, some of which were aimed, by the way—and I heard it firsthand from the parliamentarians in Norway, for example, that these acts were aimed originally at the Muslim community there and Jews were collateral damage that went along with it.

But they reverted back to traditional stereotypes of Jews as blood-sucking, vampiric figures, and these were in mainstream newspapers. So we saw that entering the mainstream of society. And I think, in essence, what we are talking about is that anti-Semitism used to be marginalized, used to be thought of as extreme. What we have seen in recent years, is through political anti-Semitism, and now through Holocaust distortion and other means, it has entered the mainstream of society with the effects that we see today where Jews throughout the world, including the Western world, feel imperiled in ways that are really, frankly, unparalleled in recent memory.

So I think the leadership question is major; I think the sense of responsibility in terms of political speech, in general, anti-Semitism in particular, is very important, but I think the leadership shown the actions of this subcommittee and yourself pave a way and a model that we hope more people will emulate.

Mr. SUOZZI. Thank you.

Ms. BURDETT. So the question you ask is so perplexing, because every public attitude survey that we see about our own country, you can look in Germany at a similar trend, the American people, the German people, people in communities are growing more tolerant of each other. More people in America today have favorable views of Jewish people than they have before, and that is true of other groups as well. But the hatred has such a microphone right now. It is hard to hear that tolerance.

And I think, you know, my colleagues have touched on a point, the Internet is anonymous. Think about what it took to bring down the Klan. It is not that the people in klavern believed our arguments that their values were not as good as ours. It is because they had to take off their hoods and show their faces, stand behind that hatred.

And, you know, our CEO, Jonathan Greenblatt, keeps reminding us that the people who used to burn crosses on front lawns are now burning up Twitter. And so my colleagues are right, it is just another platform for the same thing.

There is anger. There is a vacuum of leadership, and we are all, all of us, on both sides of this table, we are in a battle for an evidence- and a decency-based marketplace of ideas. And it goes from the global level to a very personal level. If you shoot hoops in the congressional gym with someone from the other party, you are less likely to believe it the next time one of your colleagues tells you that that guy's group is out to get you or your agenda. I say "guy," because we are in the gym in this scenario.

Mr. SUOZZI. There are women in the gym, too.

Ms. BURDETT. Oh, okay.

Mr. SUOZZI. I worked out with some Republican women today.

Ms. BURDETT. Good for you. All politics is local, as you know from being a county executive.

So your statements today, our visible partnership, communities see that. And when we can sit here as nobodies at a table and bring our expertise and give you a list of our ideas, and know that this chairman is quite likely to take all of the ideas and turn them into action and then some, that is a very powerful example for people to see.

Mr. SUOZZI. Thank you very much.

Ms. BURDETT. We are on the way.

Mr. SUOZZI. That image you gave of the idea of taking the hoods off Klan members is a very good image. Which is, you know, transparency and exposing things, sunlight is the best disinfectant, and that goes with all things in government, but certainly on this issue, exposing the people that are behind these actions and talking about it publicly is so important, and that is why it is so important that the chairman held this hearing today, and that all of you came. Thank you, again.

Mr. GOLDENBERG. Mark, I think you stirred this a little bit. One of the things we did find in working across the 10 countries—Andy and I traveled probably even more than that, as well as Stacy and I—synagogues and Jewish centers in Europe have become lightning rods for what happens geopolitically, and that should not be the case. These synagogues, these precious—they are more than infrastructure, in some cases, 100 years old, and in some cases it could be 10 years old.

These are the fabric of the nations where they sit. They are part of their fabric. And I think that that is something that we cannot allow, this continuum, evening amongst the police ranks, to believe in some of these countries that if they are attacking a synagogue, it is got to do, or associated with what is happening geopolitically 2,000, 3,000 miles away, because that is not the case. What is happening geopolitically 2,000, 3,000 miles away, is happening 2,000, 3,000 miles away.

But there are those that will use that as an excuse. We have to keep reminding people, including the security services, the national security services, these are your houses; these are your institutions; these are your synagogues; these are your schools; and your Jewish centers, and they need the same protection. They belong to you. And that is something that our collective groups are working on right now. More than a reminder, but that is about training. Thank you.

Mr. SMITH. Thank you. I would just add before yielding to Mr. Sherman, that that was the exact point that Natan Sharansky was making with his three Ds: Demonization of Israel, delegitimization, and double standard. And nowhere is that more rampant than at the United Nations, particularly the Human Rights Council, which is why, as I said in my opening, our new Ambassador to the U.N. has really drawn a line, has a zero-tolerance attitude toward that pernicious hypocrisy, which is rampant.

I have gone to the Human Rights Council myself several times, and before that, when it was called the Human Rights Commission, and was appalled to see countries whom I have great respect for Western democracies, who all of us have great respect for. They have matured, to use the word that was used earlier, democratic traditions, just joining in the parade and bashing Israel unjustly. Then that reverberates back to the attack on the synagogue, because it riles people up, and now, as was pointed out, with a click of a button, people get this misinformation, this hate, and then they act on it.

So, thank you for all of those comments.

Mr. Sherman.

Mr. SHERMAN. Mr. Chairman, thank you for letting me participate in this hearing, although as a member of the full committee, I am not a member of this subcommittee. And I want to commend you for being the author of the Global Anti-Semitism Review Act of 2004 that established the Special Envoy to Monitor and Combat Anti-Semitism——

Mr. SMITH. If the gentleman would yield? I was the House sponsor, Mr. Voinovich was the Senate sponsor. But when his bill came over, which called for a 1-year review, I offered the amendment to make it a permanent office, and then also, to establish the special envoy that Ira so thankfully led for several years.

Mr. SHERMAN. Yes.

Mr. SMITH. Just so it is clear.

Mr. SHERMAN. And I also have a personal connection to that office, since my wife was the first Deputy Special Envoy. And I take family pride in her work on the report on global anti-Semitism issued by the State Department in March of 2008.

And my first question for our panel is: We did write that report. It is almost 10 years ago. I am not saying we can write one every year, but should we be writing one every decade? Do we need another report on contemporary global anti-Semitism?

Yes, Ms. Burdett.

Ms. BURDETT. It is always a good idea to highlight issues and do special reports. If you look at the annual country reports on human rights and international religious freedom, you will see that Ira Forman and the team that is still working every day in the State Department do not get much sleep before those reports are due.

And what you have done to require these good public servants to ask every single Embassy in the world to report on anti-Semitism, when you pull that together, it is a terrific snapshot. Your legislation was game-changing, and we have eyes on the problem in places we never did.

Every 10 years it would be very, very wise to do a similar kind of report. And I know Mrs. Sherman's expertise was absolutely essential to that successful report, and you are wise to be very proud of her.

Mr. SHERMAN. Thank you.

One thing that that report does is it defines anti-Semitism, basing its definition, in large part, on the European Monitoring Centre for Racism and Xenophobia's working definition of anti-Semitism. And defining anti-Semitism is important, but especially in dealing with what I would have to describe as far left wing, or misguided left-wing anti-Semitism. On the extreme right you see references to Nazis. It is pretty obvious that it is anti-Semitic.

But you also see attacks on the Jewish people where the attacker defends it, says, oh, I am not anti-Semitic, just anti-Zionist. And there needs to be a definition that distinguishes between legitimate criticism of a Government of Israel, something most members of this panel have engaged in from time to time; and a holding Israel up to a standard that no other country is held to, or claiming that of all the countries in the world, that this is the one country that should be abolished.

What I wonder, though, is that the U.S. Department of Education doesn't have a definition of anti-Semitism, has not yet adopted the State Department definition. Does it undermine us in talking to other countries about anti-Semitism in their country that we are defining anti-Semitism by a standard that we don't apply here domestically?

Rabbi?

Rabbi BAKER. I think it is a quite pertinent question, and I would turn it around and say our ability to be a strong advocate in pressing foreign governments, as we are, to employ the working definition, whether it is in police training, whether it is in training judges and prosecutors, whether it is in monitoring anti-Semitism, would certainly be enhanced if we can cite our own example in the United States of putting it to use.

We all would hold the view, I know my organization does, when this issue first came up in the last Congress—that this working definition is a very useful educational tool. If it is a useful educational tool for the justice ministry of Austria, I would say it is a useful educational tool for the Department of Education here, which is concerned about monitoring and addressing problems of anti-Semitism on college campuses.

And if I could also speak to your first question. A U.S. global report about anti-Semitism, even if it has the same information—and, by the way, it is increasingly having much more, I think. We know what is gathered. But even if it has the same information as our own Jewish organizations might report, has an impact that is unparalleled in getting governments' attention. So having that report really allows us and everyone else to go in and to push these governments, who are now taking notice. And, finally, it has also educated, let's be candid, our own American diplomats. As Embassies have a responsibility to monitor what is going on, they are becoming more sensitive to what this is about. And, again, in these places, that definition is a very helpful tool.

Mr. SHERMAN. It has been my experience in Congress that one of the best ways to affect what people do is to ask them the right question. And by asking all of our Embassies on a continuing basis to ask their host governments what are they doing about the anti-Semitism, you drive policy in the right direction.

Mr. Weitzman?

Mr. WEITZMAN. I just would like to add as well, as you know, the 31-member nations of the International Holocaust Remembrance Alliance officially adopted a variation of the working definition of anti-Semitism. And in the negotiations and conversations with the countries leading up to that, its adoption, and my colleague, Dr. Robert Williams, from the U.S. Holocaust Memorial Museum was instrumental in assisting in this process as well, we found very often the question raised of what is the United States' position on this? We were able to refer to the State Department Web site and the documents on the Web site, but that, obviously, only dealt with external and multilateral relationships. It didn't deal with the domestic case at all.

So having this definition through the Anti-Semitism Awareness Act that is now being held up in Congress, we think would be very powerful and very strong and send a message not only to domestic constituents in the United States in terms of the people on campus, even clarifying it for the administrators. It is a tool for the administrators and the people dealing with this issue on campus, as well as for the protection of students, but it also sends a message externally as well to other countries that we are basically putting into practice what we are preaching, that our moral voice and political leadership is strong on this issue, and we feel it applies as well to the United States.

Mr. SHERMAN. And I think it undercuts our foreign policy across the board when people can point to an example where we have a standard to hold other countries to, and we refuse to impose that standard on ourselves.

The Anti-Semitism Awareness Act, I strongly support it. But, frankly, it shouldn't take that. The Department of Education has a responsibility to enforce title 6. I have worked with that Department over the last 10 years, and we got a clear statement that title 6 applies to anti-Semitism, although the statute says national origin and race, that that clearly, applies to the Jewish people as well, and to bigotry against Muslims as well.

If the Department of Education has determined that it has a responsibility to deal with anti-Semitism on campuses, it has a responsibility to have a definition of anti-Semitism. And one would wonder why they wouldn't adopt the same definition that has been adopted by so many organizations with a tweak here, with a tweak there, and, especially, why they wouldn't adopt the same definition of anti-Semitism that the State Department uses for our foreign policy.

I want to shift to Hungary. I would like to know more about this—and I am may mispronounce it—Vitezi Rend. It is my understanding that there are two rival organizations using the same name. Is there any doubt that this organization is an anti-Semitic organization?

I will ask this to Rabbi Baker, and then see if everyone else has a comment.

Rabbi BAKER. You know, this is an organization reconstituted from a prewar organization that was, certainly, anti-Semitic, Fascist, part of the supporters, followers of Admiral Horthy, and——

Mr. SHERMAN. And a pro-Nazi probe organization during World War II.

Rabbi BAKER. Exactly that. Exactly that.

So I don't know that it has much influence today in Hungary, but the reality is this is its origin, and it was around this sentiment, these ideological views, clearly, anti-Semitic, that it was re-formed.

Mr. SHERMAN. I mean, if somebody formed an organization called the Nazi Party of California, they may not publish a manifesto that is anti-Semitic, they don't need to. They name themselves the Nazi Party of California, and they have associated themselves with the Nazi Party of Germany and the role it played in world history.

So we don't have to wait for today's Vitezi Rend to publish an anti-Semitic manifesto. They have named themselves after or claim to be a continuation of an organization that was a pro-Nazi organi- zation in Hungary in the 1930s and 1940s.

Rabbi BAKER. I think they knew what they were doing when they chose their name.

Mr. SHERMAN. Yeah.

Now, I am going to get down in the weeds on this. I am told that members of this organization add a "V" as an additional middle ini- tial to show their support for the organization. Are you aware of that practice?

Rabbi BAKER. I am not.

Mr. SHERMAN. Okay.

Rabbi BAKER. But maybe the others——

Mr. SHERMAN. Gotcha.

I want to thank you for your work, thank the chairman for hold- ing these hearings, and yield back.

Mr. SMITH. Thank you.

Just a few followup questions. And thank you for your time and, again, for elaborating so well on your responses to the questions. Ms. Burdett, you made a very important, I think, observation about Latin America, which you might want to elaborate on. You point out that in Latin America, over the last few years, there has been a region-wide increase of anti-Semitic expressions and attacks directed at Jewish individuals and institutions, primarily via the Internet and social media.

You point out that Venezuela continues to be a country where state-endorsed anti-Semitism is systematic and affects government policies every day for life for Jews.

In Argentina, where the Jewish community has been the target of the infamous anti-Jewish terrorist attacks—and I did visit that community center myself and was just struck by the ongoing bro- ken-heartedness by those who run that center and the fact that the Iranian perpetrator of those crimes—the alleged, but I think the evidence is very clear—continues to be not held to account.

And then you point out the smaller countries, like Costa Rica and Uruguay, where anti-Semitism was practically negligible are now facing new challenges. And you give an example in Uruguay where a Jewish businessman was stabbed to death by a man who said that he killed a Jew following Allah's order.

You point out that your Cyber Safety Action Guide has now been translated into Spanish for dissemination there.

But if you could speak to some of this and maybe on Iran's influ- ence.

Not to get into, relitigate at this hearing the Iranian nuclear deal, which I think was egregiously flawed—and you don't have to comment on any of that, but I think it is a matter of when and not if that Iran gets nuclear weapons pursuant to those huge gaps in that agreement.

But, that said, they are getting a boatload of money. They have already gotten billions of dollars; they will get more. And that helps Hezbollah, that helps a whole lot of people. But we know that Iran is the worst, largest state sponsor of terrorism, and they certainly are anti-Semitic to the core.

And their influence in Latin America—I was in Bolivia a few years ago trying to get a Jewish businessman out of prison, Jacob Ostreicher, and had three hearings on his case alone, went down there. Our Embassy wasn't doing squat at first; they did get further involved. I went to the Palmasola Prison where he was. But the anti-Semitic view of Evo Morales and the others is palpable. And I add to that, their affection for Iran is equally disturbing.

So Iran's influence in Latin America—Venezuela, we know they are close. And Argentina, again, has this ongoing, festering sore. So if you could speak to it.

Ms. BURDETT. Well, I want to first say that the fact that this body has refused to let go of the questions around this investigation—I know there is a resolution circulating in the House, and I know your colleague from Florida, Ms. Ros-Lehtinen, who was here earlier, has been very active and engaged in this issue and looking at the Iranian connection.

Our organizations, too, thought that the JCPOA with Iran wasn't strong enough, wasn't ironclad enough.

And I think a number of the incidents that we are dealing with in the community are a result of this infectious influence. And we know that Iran practically has anti-Semitism and the export of anti-Semitism as a policy. And so, when the Supreme Leader calls Israel a cancerous tumor or when their Ministry of Culture en-dorses a Holocaust cartoon contest, that crosses every border.

And we support your efforts to shed more light on that investigation and to infuse that investigation with our assistance to expose that connection. So I think, from a governmental side, you are doing your part, and, as advocates, we are spotlighting the permeation across borders of the hate that makes those incidents possible.

Mr. SMITH. If I could, to Rabbi Baker, in your written testimony—and I appreciate your leadership on this—you point out that the chair-in-office, Steinmeier, had tried to get the definition of anti-Semitism adopted. Only one country, Russia, blocked it.

And just for the record, I have it here, without objection, I will put into the record that definition—it is very short—but also the State Department's elaboration on it, which I think gives it additional understanding.

Will a new attempt be made within the OSCE to get that definition adopted across all countries, including Russia? And if you could elaborate on that, I would appreciate it.

Rabbi BAKER. I really hope so.

There is no question that the kind of leadership that the German Foreign Minister showed was unique. And the current chair, I believe, is open, if we are able to show that there could be a consensus, to bring it up at the ministerial this December in Vienna. I think the support from Members here, Chairman Smith and those who are part of the Commission on Security and Cooperation in Europe, will also be important for this.

We need to find ways to bring Russia around on this issue. As I have noted in the past and in conversations with you, when I met with them, they explained to me they had two problems with that adoption of the definition. One concerned the views, they said, of their own Jewish experts, who they claimed opposed it, which really was not true. Another was the fact that it referenced the IHRA definition, and they said they were not members of IHRA. I asked them, "So are those the only two problems?" And they replied, "Well, for now."

So we know that it is not so much addressing them as legitimate reasons, but finding the ability to be able to say there are, not just for now but permanently, no objections. Maybe we can tweak the actual language to provide something that would be suitable. But if we can—and we will try—to secure Russian support for this or at least non-opposition, then I very much hope we can come back and perhaps succeed in December.

Mr. SMITH. One final question for me, and then I will yield to my colleague if he has any additional ones.

Obviously, Security Council Resolution 2334 was a disaster, in my opinion. It also had embedded in it language that I think is very injurious or could give amplification to the BDS movement.

And, perhaps, Mr. Weitzman, you might want to speak to that. I have met with Prince Zeid, the High Commissioner for Human Rights. And I am beyond troubled, angered, as I believe and hope—

I know you are—that compiling lists of companies that the U.N.

High Commissioner has taken it upon himself to do is a very, very dangerous precedent, somehow suggesting the illegitimacy of Israel and East Jerusalem being one and the same.

Any final determination between the Palestinians and Israelis, as we all have said a thousand times, needs to be negotiated between the two entities. To have this, increasingly, imposition of an outcome dictated by the United Nations and its bureaucracy is troubling, but when there is also an economic threat posed by BDS, that raises it even further. And that will have more impact, in my opinion, in Europe than it will here, although it will impact us here as well, as those companies are listed that do business in areas that are in contention with United Nations.

And maybe if you could just elaborate too on that there are right-wing and there are left-wing strong manifestations of anti-Semitism. We see it. I guess what came out, Rabbi Baker, to me, in those very early meetings in Vienna and then Berlin and then followup meetings was hatred from the left and the right. I remember when we were pushing Holocaust remembrance in France, it was the teachers union and the leftists who were most adamantly opposed to any kind of teaching of students of the Holocaust. So the left and the right has shame on its face, in my opinion, the extreme left and the extreme right.

But BDS is also something that the left is pushing. Maybe you might want to speak to that as well.

66

Mr. WEITZMAN. Thank you.

In regards to the United Nations, I think one of the things that we have seen is really the vigorous pushback by Ambassador Haley in leading the U.S. delegation to make it very clear that we will not tolerate crossing a certain line of what is really acceptable political discourse and what is not.

And we were very encouraged by the reaction of the Secretary-General in not only rejecting the flawed report that came out that linked Israel to apartheid practices but actually taking it down from the U.N. Web site, which already actually caused at least one diplomat to resign in protest over it. But it was really unprecedented, and we are very cheered that the Secretary-General took a strong step on that. And we hope that that is showing a little bit of a shift back to a more rational and decent approach by the U.N.

I think, in terms of BDS, one of the things that we have seen is that, again, a number of States in the United States, as well as a number of cities, have passed laws against BDS recently, over the past year or so, which are something that I think will strengthen the backbone, even though it wasn't necessarily, I think, a lot of cases that this was not necessarily a practical step as much as an expression of political will and an expression of common belief that BDS is not only against Israel and not only anti-Semitic but is fundamentally un-American. It challenges freedom of speech, freedom of opinion, and, as such, I think most Americans would reject it instinctively.

What happens in Europe, again, I think the United States can play a very strong role in positioning itself as a leader against BDS and in making sure that, given the prominence of the U.S. industries, that BDS fails, as it has failed in so many other places.

I will say, in terms of right-wing and left-wing extremism, one of the points that I would like to just make briefly is that there has been a sea change in right-wing extremism in the United States over the past generation or so.

People had referred to the Klan, and if you look back at Klan history and documents, they originally came about, and even through the 1960s and the civil rights period, they claimed fealty to a vision, a flawed and totally historically inaccurate, but idealized vision, of the United States as an antebellum Southern vision of a place where slavery and religious persecution were embedded in the Constitution and, thus, were American ideals.

The generation that we have starting in the later part of the 20th century is a generation of extremists who see themselves at war with the United States. They consider the U.S. Government Zionist-occupied government territory. And that is one of the reasons why they are so ready to go into violent acts, because, to them, a state of war already exists with the Jews who control the U.S. Government and people down to postal workers who have been murdered because they wore a government uniform.

That has then translated it into the rhetoric that we see sometimes on the extremes of the alt-right and so on, who consider themselves at war with established political institutions and political norms in the U.S. And I think that is one of the things that we have to recognize, the shift between the traditional extremism and the new status that we have now.

And, of course, again, the left-wing extremism is very often filtered through traditional—going back to Communist opposition to Israel, to opposition to Jews as a distinct religion, both of which are fundamentally opposed by communism, and even the erasure of Jews from history, as the infamous plaque at Babi Yar under Communists basically talked about the victims of fascism in a generic sense, at Auschwitz as well, taking away and erasing the specificity of the Jewish experience in that period.

Rabbi BAKER. Just to be very brief, I think one of the phenomena of anti-Semitism is that it can link haters from all across the spectrum who literally have nothing else in common. It almost defies any rational understanding.

We have come to see and expect it as part of a right-wing, xenophobic ideology. It has traditionally been there in Europe, and in almost all of these nationalist parties anti-Semitism is a piece of it.

At the same time—and, again, I reference having been relatively recently in Sweden—you have now a growth, it was pointed out to us, of these—in many cases, they are minority groups, hip-hop and rap artists engaged in concerts to combat racism that use overtly anti-Semitic language in their lyrics. So how do you square this?

The fact is it is a phenomenon we are seeing not only, as Mark has indicated, from the historical notions of what communism or socialist movements may have done, but even in what would almost be a kind of "post-movement" Europe today, where, still, figures on the left—they may be literary figures, musical figures, or others—have folded in this—again, it may start as anti-Zionism, but it often comes full-blown as an anti-Semitism with all of those negative stereotypes of Jews. It is there.

Mr. SMITH. That concludes the hearing.

I want to thank you again for your extraordinary leadership, each of you, and for giving us the benefit as a subcommittee and, by extension, the Congress—because we will share this widely with the leadership, especially your testimonies today. And as the record is obviously produced, we will get that out to key policymakers as well. Because, again, you have provided a treasure trove of insight and expectation as well as the experience. And past is prologue; we need to learn from the past and also face these new challenges as they emerge.

So thank you so very, very much.

The hearing is adjourned.

[Whereupon, at 12:20 p.m., the subcommittee was adjourned.]

APPENDIX

MATERIAL SUBMITTED FOR THE RECORD

SUBCOMMITTEE HEARING NOTICE
COMMITTEE ON FOREIGN AFFAIRS
U.S. HOUSE OF REPRESENTATIVES
WASHINGTON, DC 20515-6128

Subcommittee on Africa, Global Health, Global Human Rights, and International Organizations
Christopher H. Smith (R-NJ), Chairman

March 22, 2017

TO: MEMBERS OF THE COMMITTEE ON FOREIGN AFFAIRS

You are respectfully requested to attend an OPEN hearing of the Committee on Foreign Affairs, to be held by the Subcommittee on Africa, Global Health, Global Human Rights, and International Organizations in Room 2172 of the Rayburn House Office Building (and available live on the Committee website at http://www.ForeignAffairs.house.gov):

DATE: Wednesday, March 22, 2017

TIME: 10:00 a.m.

SUBJECT: Anti-Semitism Across Borders

WITNESSES: Mr. Paul Goldenberg
                   National Director
                   Secure Community Network

                   Rabbi Andrew Baker
                   Personal Representative on Combating Anti-Semitism
                   Office of the Chairperson-in-Office
                   Organization for Security and Co-operation in Europe

                   Mr. Mark Weitzman
                   Director of Government Affairs
                   Simon Wiesenthal Center

                   Ms. Stacy Burdett
                   Vice President
                   Government Relations, Advocacy, and Community Engagement
                   Anti-Defamation League

By Direction of the Chairman

The Committee on Foreign Affairs seeks to make its facilities accessible to persons with disabilities. If you are in need of special accommodations, please call 202/225-5021 at least four business days in advance of the event, whenever practicable. Questions with regard to special accommodations in general (including availability of Committee materials in alternative formats and assistive listening devices) may be directed to the Committee.

COMMITTEE ON FOREIGN AFFAIRS

MINUTES OF SUBCOMMITTEE ON *Africa, Global Health, Global Human Rights, and International Organizations* HEARING

Day_ *Wednesday*_ Date_ *March 22, 2017*_ Room_ *2172 Rayburn HOB*_

Starting Time_ *10:03 p.m.*_ Ending Time_ *12:20 p.m.*_

Recesses | *0* | (___to___)(___to___)(___to___)(___to___)(___to___)(___to___)

Presiding Member(s)

Rep. Chris Smith, Rep. Dan Donovan

Check all of the following that apply:

Open Session ☑
Executive (closed) Session ☐
Televised ☑

Electronically Recorded (taped) ☑
Stenographic Record ☑

TITLE OF HEARING:

Anti-Semitism Across Borders

SUBCOMMITTEE MEMBERS PRESENT:

Rep. Karen Bass, Rep. Tom Suozzi

NON-SUBCOMMITTEE MEMBERS PRESENT: *(Mark with an * if they are not members of full committee.)*

Rep. Bradley S. Schneider, Rep. Ileana Ros-Lehtinen, Rep. Brad Sherman

HEARING WITNESSES: Same as meeting notice attached? Yes ☑ No ☐
(If "no", please list below and include title, agency, department, or organization.)

STATEMENTS FOR THE RECORD: *(List any statements submitted for the record.)*

List of cities with no reports of hate crimes, submitted by Ms. Stacy Burdett
Wisenthal Center's Overview of Digital Terrorism and Hate, submitted by Rep. Chris Smith
State Department definition and examples of anti-Semitism, submitted by Rep. Chris Smith
ADL and HRF Scorecard on Hate Crime Response in the OSCE Region, submitted by Ms. Stacy Burdett
Statement of the Union of Orthodox Jewish Congregations of America, submitted by Rep. Chris Smith
Statement of the B'nai B'rith International, submitted by Rep. Chris Smith

TIME SCHEDULED TO RECONVENE _____
or
TIME ADJOURNED_ *12:20 p.m.*_

_____
Subcommittee Staff Associate

MATERIAL SUBMITTED FOR THE RECORD BY MS. STACY BURDETT, VICE PRESIDENT, GOVERNMENT RELATIONS, ADVOCACY, AND COMMUNITY ENGAGEMENT, ANTI-DEFAMATION LEAGUE

FBI 2015 HCSA Did Not Report (DNR) and Zero Reported Agencies

	Group 1 DNR					
	City	Population (2015)	2015 Incidents	2014 Incidents	2013 Incidents	2012 Incidents
1	Honolulu, HI	999,307	DNR	DNR	DNR	DNR
2	Jacksonville, FL	867,258	DNR	0	5	4
3	Portland, OR	628,192	DNR	DNR	6	7
4	Miami, FL	437,969	DNR	0	0	0
5	Tampa, FL	364,383	DNR	0	0	0
6	Orlando, FL*	268,438	DNR	5	2	3
7	St. Petersburg, FL	255,821	DNR	0	1	0

	Group 2 DNR					
	City	Population (2015)	2015 Incidents	2014 Incidents	2013 Incidents	2012 Incidents
1	Hialeah, FL	238,132	DNR	0	0	0
2	Columbus, GA*	203,778	DNR	DNR	0	2
3	Huntsville, AL*	190,106	DNR	DNR	0	2
4	Fort Lauderdale, FL	178,598	DNR	0	0	1
5	Cape Coral, FL	173,844	DNR	1	0	1
6	Jackson, MS	170,508	DNR	0	0	DNR
7	Hollywood, FL	149,822	DNR	0	0	0
8	Miramar, FL	138,330	DNR	1	1	3
9	Gresham, OR	110,901	DNR	DNR	DNR	DNR
10	Pompano Beach, FL	107,656	DNR	0	DNR	DNR
11	Lakeland, FL*	103,498	DNR	0	0	1
12	Las Cruces, NM*	102,227	DNR	DNR	DNR	DNR
13	Hillsboro, OR	101,206	DNR	DNR	DNR	DNR
14	Davie, FL	100,612	DNR	0	0	0

	Group 1 Reported Zero					
	City	Population (2015)	2015 Incidents	2014 Incidents	2013 Incidents	2012 Incidents
1	Tulsa, OK*	401,520	0	0	0	DNR
2	Arlington, TX	387,565	0	0	0	DNR
3	Anaheim, CA	349,471	0	0	0	1
4	Newark, NJ	280,888	0	5	3	DNR
5	Laredo, TX*	256,280	0	0	0	0
6	Mobile, AL	250,346	0	0	0	DNR

	Group 2 Reported Zero					
	City	Population (2015)	2015 Incidents	2014 Incidents	2013 Incidents	2012 Incidents
1	Lubbock, TX*	247,271	0	1	0	0
2	Winston-Salem, NC	241,631	0	0	0	1
3	Savannah-Chatham Metro, GA*	240,178	0	0	0	0
4	Garland, TX	237,593	0	1	2	DNR
5	Irving, TX	236,465	0	0	0	DNR
6	Baton Rouge, LA*	228,727	0	DNR	DNR	DNR
7	Fontana, CA	206,982	0	3	1	0
8	Montgomery, AL*	199,139	0	DNR	DNR	DNR
9	Amarillo, TX*	198,770	0	0	0	1

Bolded cities with an FBI Field Office
Asterisked (*) cities with an FBI Resident Agency

More information about ADL's resources on hate violence can be found at the League's Website: www.adl.org
©Anti-Defamation League 2016

	City	Population (2015)	2015 Incidents	2014 Incidents	2013 Incidents	2012 Incidents
10	**Little Rock, AR**	198,217	0	0	0	0
11	Brownsville, TX*	184,941	0	0	0	0
12	Tempe, AZ	175,556	0	2	3	5
13	Sioux Falls, SD*	172,313	0	2	4	15
14	Peoria, AZ	170,222	0	0	0	DNR
15	Corona, CA	163,633	0	0	1	3
16	Cary, NC	160,291	0	0	0	0
17	Pasadena, TX	154,986	0	0	1	0
18	Pomona, CA	154,410	0	2	0	4
19	Sunnyvale, CA	152,443	0	1	1	3
20	Lakewood, CO	151,311	0	1	4	2
21	Kansas City, KS	150,370	0	1	0	DNR
22	Joliet, IL	147,991	0	1	0	1
23	Naperville, IL	147,101	0	DNR	0	0
24	Paterson, NJ	146,588	0	0	0	0
25	Mesquite, TX	145,569	0	0	0	0
26	Syracuse, NY*	144,027	0	0	0	0
27	McAllen, TX*	140,593	0	0	1	0
28	Killeen, TX	140,497	0	1	0	0
29	Olathe, KS	134,830	0	0	0	DNR
30	Thornton, CO	133,188	0	0	3	0
31	Midland, TX*	132,625	0	0	0	0
32	Sterling Heights, MI	132,255	0	0	0	4
33	Waco, TX*	131,413	0	0	0	0
34	Elizabeth, NJ	129,364	0	0	0	0
35	Surprise, AZ	128,525	0	0	0	0
36	Lafayette, LA*	127,273	0	0	0	0
37	Murfreesboro, TN	123,994	0	0	1	2
38	Santa Clara, CA	123,562	0	0	2	0
39	Abilene, TX*	121,764	0	0	0	0
40	Vallejo, CA	121,257	0	0	2	2
41	Evansville, IN*	120,414	0	0	0	DNR
42	Allentown, PA*	119,335	0	1	DNR	DNR
43	Peoria, AL	116,066	0	DNR	DNR	DNR
44	Round Rock, TX	115,955	0	0	0	DNR
45	Provo, UT	115,294	0	0	1	2
46	Downey, CA	114,754	0	0	0	1
47	Carlsbad, CA	113,972	0	0	3	0
48	Westminster, CO	113,547	0	0	1	1
49	Costa Mesa, CA	113,477	0	0	1	0
50	Inglewood, CA	112,450	0	1	0	1
51	Richardson, TX	111,008	0	2	0	DNR
52	Murrieta, CA	109,495	0	1	5	2
53	Waterbury, CT	109,044	0	4	6	6
54	Broken Arrow, OK	106,145	0	0	1	DNR
55	College Station, TX	105,855	0	1	DNR	DNR
56	Wichita Falls, TX*	105,186	0	2	0	DNR
57	Santa Maria, CA*	104,355	0	0	1	1
58	Sandy Springs, GA	103,898	0	0	0	0
59	Davenport, IA	103,082	0	0	0	0
60	Kenosha, WI	100,038	0	0	0	0

Bolded cities with an FBI Field Office
Asterisked (*) cities with an FBI Resident Agency
Updated November 2016
Compiled by the Anti-Defamation League's Washington Office from information collected by the FBI:
http://www.fbi.gov/about-us/investigate/civilrights/hate_crimes/
More information about ADL's resources on hate violence can be found at the League's Website: www.adl.org
©Anti-Defamation League 2016

MATERIAL SUBMITTED FOR THE RECORD BY MS. STACY BURDETT, VICE PRESIDENT, GOVERNMENT RELATIONS, ADVOCACY, AND COMMUNITY ENGAGEMENT, ANTI-DEFAMATION LEAGUE

Anti-Defamation League»

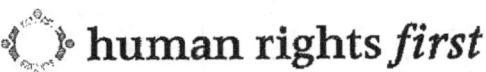

Scorecard on Hate Crime Response in the OSCE Region
Gaps in Data Collection and Responses

November 30, 2016

Overview

Against a backdrop of increasing hateful rhetoric in the public space, as well as acts of discrimination and hate crimes, the Organization for Security and Cooperation in Europe's (OSCE) Office for Democratic Institutions and Human Rights (ODIHR) released its annual report on hate crimes in the OSCE region.[1] This report is essential to understanding hate crimes and crafting effective policy responses.

Every year since 2009, ODIHR releases this report on the International Day for Tolerance, and every year since 2010, Human Rights First and the Anti-Defamation League (ADL) analyze ODIHR's findings and rate countries' performances in keeping their commitment to track and report hate crimes.

This year in particular demonstrates why this work is critical. Xenophobic and hateful rhetoric dominated political discourse is several OSCE participating States, and this rhetoric was often matched with hate-inspired violence.

What leaders say matters, and often those committing hate crimes use the rhetoric of politicians to legitimize their violence. From the Brexit campaign in the United Kingdom, to the refugee referendum in Hungary, to the U.S. presidential election, toxic rhetoric has infected citizens of these countries and emboldened those who seek to spread hate and violence.

ODIHR's annual report is an important tool in understanding the nature and frequency of hate crimes across the OSCE region. However, its utility is minimized when participating States do not collect or report data, provide insufficient data, or fail to submit data by the ODIHR deadline. Data may be insufficient if it records an implausibly low level of hate crimes or when it is not disaggregated by bias motivation.

The data from this year's report, covering 2015, demonstrates that participating **States continue to fail, or barely pass, in upholding their commitments to prevent and combat hate crime.** In the current environment, with the refugee crisis, the rise of far-right parties and movements espousing hatred, and a rise in bias-motivated incidents throughout the region, there **is an urgent need for prevention, data collection, and reporting to receive higher priority.**

The Impact of Hate Violence

Violent hate crimes have a uniquely serious impact on victims and their communities, and must be viewed as a serious human rights violation.[2] When a bias-motivated crime is committed, the victim's entire community feels victimized, vulnerable, fearful, isolated, and unprotected by the law.

These crimes merit special attention. Regrettably, the overwhelming majority of the OSCE's 57 participating States are not doing everything they can to ensure they receive it.

Hate crimes violate the right to equality and non-discrimination because of their bias-motivation. The fear and intimidation these crimes are meant to cause undermine the right to free expression and religion. They inhibit the right of the targeted groups to participate fully in political, social, and cultural life. The injustice is magnified if these crimes are not documented or prosecuted fully.

The OSCE is built on a vision that human rights are essential to security. Effectively monitoring, prosecuting, and preventing hate crimes is essential to that vision. 2015 data released from the OSCE's ODIHR shows that

In March 2017, the Simon Wiesenthal Center released Vol 19 of Digital Terrorism and Hate, its interactive overview of online extremism. The report (available at www.digitalhate.net) is comprised of over 700 individual entries, includes over 50 videos and hundreds of PDF attachments detailing online extremism and the newest online trends in 2017.

Digital Terrorism and Hate is broken into three major categories including a section on Terrorism, a Geographic breakdown of sites around the world and a Strategies section explaining how the Internet is used by extremists. Each major category has two additional levels of sub-categories.

The Terrorism section outlines sites used for recruiting, an instructional category showing how potential terrorists receive information on explosives, bomb-making and guerilla tactics, and a who's who of online terrorist groups. The support section previews the ever-growing list of digital magazines distributed by Al Qaeda, ISIS, Al Shabaab Mujahideen and other groups around the world.

The Strategies section contains entries detailing the new platforms used by both terrorists and hate groups. These new platforms include discussion groups such as 8chan, Disqus and Voat, blogging sites such as GAB and encrypted messaging sites including Telegram, Kik, Surespot and Signal Messenger.

The Geographic section, broken down by region, includes the growth of the alt-Right in the United States, connections to groups in Europe, Asia and Latin America, and a Transnational section detailing groups operating in multiple locations.

Throughout all sections of the report, the extensive use of social media is highlighted, including traditional sites such as Facebook, Twitter and YouTube, and the always expanding list of new sites used by extremists. From 35-40 online hate sites in 1995, the Simon Wiesenthal Center has chronicled the growth of online Extremism and Terrorism to unprecedented levels in 2017. The rapid growth of social networking sites has made it virtually impossible count the number of sites currently online. In 2015 the Simon Wiesenthal Center began issuing a Report Card that reflects how social networking companies are dealing with unprecedented threat posed by online terrorists and extremists.

2017 SIMON WIESENTHAL CENTER

SOCIAL MEDIA grades

DIGITAL TERRORISM + HATE Report Card

	TERRORISM	HATE
FACEBOOK	A-	B-
TWITTER	B-↑	C↑
GOOGLE / YOU TUBE	C-↓	D

INSTAGRAM	B+↓	VK.COM	D↑
PINTEREST	C+	REDDIT	C-
WORDPRESS	D-	SOUNDCLOUD	D↓
GOOGLE+	C-↓	8CHAN	F
TUMBLR	C↓	GAB	F
ASK.FM	B+		

MESSAGING APPS

TELEGRAM	B-↓
KIK	D
SURESPOT	F
SNAPCHAT	incomplete

MATERIAL SUBMITTED FOR THE RECORD BY THE HONORABLE CHRISTOPHER H. SMITH, A REPRESENTATIVE IN CONGRESS FROM THE STATE OF NEW JERSEY, AND CHAIRMAN, SUBCOMMITTEE ON AFRICA, GLOBAL HEALTH, GLOBAL HUMAN RIGHTS, AND INTERNATIONAL ORGANIZATIONS

Defining Anti-Semitism
January 20, 2017

"Anti-Semitism is a certain perception of Jews, which may be expressed as hatred toward Jews. Rhetorical and physical manifestations of anti-Semitism are directed toward Jewish or non-Jewish individuals and/or their property, toward Jewish community institutions and religious facilities." -- Working Definition of Anti-Semitism by the European Monitoring Center on Racism and Xenophobia

Contemporary Examples of Anti-Semitism

- Calling for, aiding, or justifying the killing or harming of Jews (often in the name of a radical ideology or an extremist view of religion).
- Making mendacious, dehumanizing, demonizing, or stereotypical allegations about Jews as such or the power of Jews as a collective—especially but not exclusively, the myth about a world Jewish conspiracy or of Jews controlling the media, economy, government or other societal institutions.
- Accusing Jews as a people of being responsible for real or imagined wrongdoing committed by a single Jewish person or group, the state of Israel, or even for acts committed by non-Jews.
- Accusing the Jews as a people, or Israel as a state, of inventing or exaggerating the Holocaust.
- Accusing Jewish citizens of being more loyal to Israel, or to the alleged priorities of Jews worldwide, than to the interest of their own nations.

What is Anti-Semitism Relative to Israel?

EXAMPLES of the ways in which anti-Semitism manifests itself with regard to the state of Israel, taking into account the overall context could include:

DEMONIZE ISRAEL:

- Using the symbols and images associated with classic anti-Semitism to characterize Israel or Israelis
- Drawing comparisons of contemporary Israeli policy to that of the Nazis
- Blaming Israel for all inter-religious or political tensions

DOUBLE STANDARD FOR ISRAEL:

- Applying double standards by requiring of it a behavior not expected or demanded of any other democratic nation
- Multilateral organizations focusing on Israel only for peace or human rights investigations

DELEGITIMIZE ISRAEL:

- Denying the Jewish people their right to self-determination, and denying Israel the right to exist

However, criticism of Israel similar to that leveled against any other country cannot be regarded as anti-Semitic.

MATERIAL SUBMITTED FOR THE RECORD BY THE HONORABLE CHRISTOPHER H. SMITH, A REPRESENTATIVE IN CONGRESS FROM THE STATE OF NEW JERSEY, AND CHAIRMAN, SUBCOMMITTEE ON AFRICA, GLOBAL HEALTH, GLOBAL HUMAN RIGHTS, AND INTERNATIONAL ORGANIZATIONS

UNION OF ORTHODOX JEWISH CONGREGATIONS OF AMERICA

March 22, 2017

MARK (MOISHE) BANE
President

ALLEN FAGIN
Executive Vice President

JERRY WOLASKY
Chairman, Advocacy

NATHAN J. DIAMENT
Executive Director

MAURY LITWACK
Director of State
Political Affairs

HOWARD FRIEDMAN
Chairman, Board of Directors

The Honorable Chris Smith
United States Congress

Dear Representative Smith:

On behalf of the Union of Orthodox Jewish Congregations of America (Orthodox Union)—the nation's largest Orthodox Jewish umbrella organization—we thank you and members of the House Committee on Foreign Affairs, Subcommittee on Africa, Global Health, Global Human Rights, and International Organizations for holding today's hearing on "Anti-Semitism Across Borders." The topic is timely-- since January, Jewish Community Centers, Day Schools, Synagogues, and offices have received 165 bomb threats from New York to San Francisco and in February, Jewish cemeteries in Pennsylvania and Missouri were vandalized.

The Orthodox Union appreciates the action of law enforcement officials, Congress, and the FBI in responding to these threats. We join Congress in calling on the FBI and other security agencies to find the individuals or organizations behind these threats, bring them to justice, and deter such threats in the future. In a nation founded on religious freedom, incidents of anti-Semitism are absolutely unacceptable.

Many of the Orthodox Union member synagogues and schools—and Jewish organizations nationwide—have security measures and best practices for responding to threats in place. We will continue to implement procedures and provide the safest environment possible for our community. As Congress examines this issue and makes recommendations for what needs to be done, we encourage federal law enforcement agencies to quickly implement recommended measures.

In addition, we call on relevant agencies to continue funding security measures, such as the Department of Homeland Security's Nonprofit Security Grant Program (NSGP). In 2005, the effort to create the NSGP was spearheaded by the Orthodox Union (together with the Jewish Federations of North America) and the support of many coalition partners and bipartisan leaders in Congress.

Since that time, Congress has appropriated nearly $200 million for the NSGP, and awarded over 2,000 grants to at-risk nonprofit organizations, including Jewish Community Centers, Synagogues, and Jewish Day Schools. These grants have provided for the acquisition and installation of critical security improvements including fencing, lighting, surveillance, metal detection equipment, blast proofing doors, windows and more at hundreds of synagogues and schools in the United States. The continued operation and funding of the NSGP is essential, as it will not only keep our community safer, but will be a statement of solidarity and support in the face of anti-Semitic threats.

Sincerely,

Nathan J. Diament

OU Advocacy is the non-partisan public policy and advocacy arm of the Orthodox Union; the nation's largest Orthodox Jewish umbrella organization founded in 1898.

820 FIRST STREET, NE, SUITE 730 | WASHINGTON, D.C. 20002 | TEL: 202.513.6484 | FAX: 202.513.6497 | WWW.OUADVOCACY.ORG

MATERIAL SUBMITTED FOR THE RECORD BY THE HONORABLE CHRISTOPHER H. SMITH, A REPRESENTATIVE IN CONGRESS FROM THE STATE OF NEW JERSEY, AND CHAIRMAN, SUBCOMMITTEE ON AFRICA, GLOBAL HEALTH, GLOBAL HUMAN RIGHTS, AND INTERNATIONAL ORGANIZATIONS

Written testimony for the record

Eric Fusfield
Director of Legislative Affairs
Deputy Director, International Center for Human Rights and Public Policy
B'nai B'rith International

Hearing: Anti-Semitism Across Borders
House of Representatives
Committee on Foreign Affairs
Subcommittee on Africa, Global Health, Global Human Rights, and International Organizations
Washington, D.C.
March 22, 2017

B'nai B'rith International, representing more than 100,000 members and supporters around the world, would like to thank Chairman Smith, Ranking Member Bass, and the other members of the Subcommittee for convening this hearing and for their strong leadership in addressing the serious problem of global anti-Semitism. The role of the United States Congress is indispensable in the ongoing struggle against anti-Semitism and the related problem of anti-Israel hatred.

Few issues have generated as much attention or distress in the contemporary Jewish world as the rise of anti-Semitism. Tragically, 17 years after the outbreak of the second Intifada in the Middle East, evidence of rising or sustained levels of anti-Semitism continues to manifest itself around the globe. In the past year, for example:

- Belgian elementary school students bullied a Jewish classmate, whom they sprayed with deodorant while he was showering at school to simulate Nazi gas chambers.

- Assailants desecrated 14 gravestones at a Jewish cemetery in Manchester, England, leaving the Jewish population shaken.

- In the Netherlands around the same time, a group of students yelled, "Together we'll burn the Jews, because Jews burn the best" at a high school graduation gala in Schijndel, a town 70 miles outside of Amsterdam.

- In Paysandu, Uruguay, a man shouting "Allah akbar" stabbed a Jewish businessman to death and injured the victim's son. The murderer told authorities that he "killed a Jew following Allah's order."

- In Rio de Janeiro, Brazil, three swastikas were found on walls in a Jewish neighborhood.

- In Newton, Massachusetts, students at a Catholic high school chanted "You killed Jesus" to the predominantly Jewish fan base of Newton North High School. Two weeks earlier, the words "Burn the Jews appeared on a bathroom wall in Newton Middle School.

- Students for Justice in Palestine, a group that supports the Boycott, Divestment, and Sanctions (BDS) movement, has been posting "eviction notices" on the dorm room doors of Jewish university students, demanding that they vacate their rooms within three days or have their property destroyed.

The problem has been most acute in Europe, where anti-Semitism has reasserted itself as a cultural virus and even gained potency in many respects. On the continent that gave rise to the Holocaust, the ugly specter of anti-Semitism has further tarnished European society for much of the past 17 years, posing the greatest threat to face the Jewish community at any point since World War II.

It has long been a fear of Jews and other supporters of Israel that the generation of European politicians who grew up either during the war or in its immediate aftermath would give way to a younger generation for whom the Holocaust was merely a distant historical episode, its lessons substantially faded, if not forgotten altogether. This helps explain the easy embrace of anti-Semitic attitudes—taboo for many years after the war, but no longer, apparently. Also compromised is the bedrock understanding of the crucial importance of Israel's existence, as some critics of the Jewish state have asserted that Israel's very right to exist must be put into question as a result of its policies, whereas no other state in the world—whether democracy or dictatorship—would ever have its right of sovereignty challenged on the grounds of a policy or an action.

While the Jewish state has been a preferred target of anti-Semites in the 21st century, the Jewish *religion* also appears to be coming increasingly under assault. Last year the Danish Medical Association considered proposing a legal ban on circumcision for children under the age of 18. This follows a history of similar opposition to Jewish ritual practices across Europe – sometimes on the basis of a humanitarian argument, but nonetheless with the result of impinging on Jewish laws and customs that go to the core of Jewish identity. Germany, Austria, and Switzerland have at times advanced measures limiting circumcision. The Danish Medical Association's deliberations provide further evidence of how hostile rhetoric from the media and politicians in Scandinavia has intensified the stigma against circumcision in that region. In 2013, the Council of Europe easily passed a resolution denouncing circumcision as "a violation of the physical integrity of children." Meanwhile, the practice of kosher ritual slaughter, or shechita, is banned in four European countries; attempts to lift the prohibition in Switzerland resulted in an anti-Semitic backlash. During a similar debate in Norway, a parliamentarian once declared that if the Jews didn't like the ban, "Let them go somewhere else."

One strategy employed by several European governments to combat hatred, unthinkable here in the United States with our First Amendment freedoms, has been a ban on Nazi symbols and tropes. In Germany, the swastika and the Heil Hitler salute are both illegal, as is denial of the Holocaust. But neo-Nazi parties such as the National Democratic Party are allowed to publicly air their views as long as they don't hew too closely to the platform of the Third Reich.

This structured compromise between Germany's sense of obligation to acknowledge its Nazi-era past while upholding the values of a contemporary liberal democracy reflects a policy born out of the country's unique historical and political context. Critics might argue that any suppression of hate speech ultimately leads to a backlash of sorts and only stokes the embers of intolerance. But defenders of Germany's legal framework would argue that it balances essential freedoms against the dangers of extremism left unchecked.

Another venue in which the impulse to impose legal restraints is pitted against the imperative to uphold free speech is the Internet. Given that the U.S., with our First Amendment, essentially is a safe-haven for virtually all Web content, removing material or shutting down a web site in Europe or Canada through legal channels cannot ensure that the contents will be permanently censored. The global reach of the Internet makes such an outcome far more difficult to attain. Many see prosecution of Internet speech in one country as a futile gesture when the speech can re-appear on the Internet almost instantaneously, hosted by an Internet service provider in the United States. These dynamics underscore the importance of education and counter-speech, given the easy access to hate speech on the Internet and the fact that young people are such dedicated users of the medium. And the potential role of Internet service providers and search engines to voluntarily block hateful content can significantly change the equation in the campaign against hate speech by making access to mainstream hosts more elusive.

One country of growing concern is Poland, a nation rich in Jewish heritage but with few remaining Jewish residents. A new University of Warsaw study has revealed a spike in anti-Semitic attitudes in Poland over the past three years, with hate speech appearing more frequently on TV and the Internet. This is happening at a time when Poland's government has shown an unwillingness to acknowledge the country's role during the Holocaust, in which some Poles were complicit in the murder of Jews. On a visit to Israel last fall, Prime Minister Beata Szydło referred to World War II, saying: "Today Poland and Israel are united by our history, common fates, which were so brutally interrupted by Nazi invaders." She added, "There is understanding and a full will to cooperate and clearly state who was the invader, who was the executioner and who was the victim." In her historical framework, Jews and Poles were equally victimized, while the Nazis were the sole perpetrators.

Hungary has also proven deeply worrisome, as in recent years it has witnessed the rise of the xenophobic and anti-Semitic Jobbik party, which has called for the creation of a list of Jewish public officials, repeated the historic "blood libel" against Jewish, and labeled Jews a "national security risk." An increase in violence against Jewish individuals and institutions and the proliferation of anti-Semitic materials in the media and the Internet has mirrored the rise of anti-Semitic public opinion, include the use of traditional stereotypes. Furthermore, the government has attempted to rehabilitate and glorify World War II-era figures who were openly anti-Semitic and pro-fascist.

The Jewish community of France continues to feel the pressure of living in a country where attacks on Jewish institutions and individuals have occurred with disturbing frequency. Roughly 8,000 French Jews immigrated to Israel in 2015, a record number. The previous year, approximately 7,000 French Jews made aliyah, more than double the number in 2013. Rising anti-Semitism has been a key factor behind the exodus of Jews from France in recent years, exemplified by the terror attack in January 2015 at a kosher supermarket in Paris.

It is important to acknowledge the significant work of the Organization for Security and Cooperation in Europe (OSCE), which has taken steps to combat anti-Semitism and the related issues of racism and xenophobia. A series of OSCE conferences, most notably in Berlin in 2004 and a 10th anniversary gathering in 2014, have focused exclusively or primarily on anti-Semitism and yielded some positive results. It was therefore of particular note that the historic 2004 Berlin Declaration, which provided a blueprint for combating hate crimes against Jewish individuals and institutions, specifically addressed the growing problem of anti-Semitic attacks being committed by opponents of Israel's policies toward the Palestinians. The passage stating that "international developments or political issues, including those in Israel or elsewhere in the Middle East, never justify anti-Semitism" should be a wake-up call to those who try to justify hate crimes with politics.

Furthermore, the Berlin Declaration issued a series of recommendations for the governments of Europe, North America, and the former Soviet Union to follow in combating anti-Semitism, including an informal exchange of "best practices" between nations; government support for anti-hate programs; systematic data collection on anti-Semitic acts; assistance in facilitating the prosecution of anti-Semitic crimes; and the promotion of academic exchange and educational programs.

In the tradition of the OSCE Berlin Conference, governments everywhere should comply with their moral and legal obligations to combat anti-Semitism and other forms of intolerance.

- Countries should compile comprehensive statistical information relevant to hate-motivated crimes; too few governments have done so until now.

- Governments should adopt and fully enforce domestic legislation aimed at curbing intolerance, as well as implementing effective monitoring procedures.

- Countries should develop Holocaust education programs that underscore the distinct nature of anti-Semitism and link the historical struggle against Nazism to the contemporary battle against anti-Semitism.

- Governments should convene multilateral gatherings to share best practices and to pressure other governments to comply with their obligations in combating intolerance.

- Public officials must forcefully denounce and stigmatize anti-Semitism and other forms of intolerance and underscore the principle that political events in the Middle East or elsewhere never justify anti-Semitism.

Progress in these spheres will require a continuation of the collaborative effort of friendly countries and NGOs in order for the promise of the Berlin Conference to be realized in a serious way. Education ministers and justice ministers, for example, should regularly meet in multilateral fora to develop an ongoing form of cooperation on matters related to anti-Semitism and hate crimes. And governments should actively support the important work of the International Holocaust Remembrance Alliance.

Last year the International Holocaust Remembrance Alliance (IHRA) adopted a working definition of anti-Semitism, stating that the ways in which anti-Israel rhetoric crosses the line into anti-Semitism "include: (1) Denying the Jewish people their right to self-determination, e.g., by claiming that the existence of a State of Israel is a racist endeavor; (2) Applying double standards by requiring of it a behavior not expected or demanded of any other democratic nation; (3) Using the symbols and images associated with classic anti-Semitism (e.g., claims of Jews killing Jesus or blood libel) to characterize Israel or Israelis; (4) Drawing comparisons of contemporary Israeli policy to that of the Nazis; (5) Holding Jews collectively responsible for actions of the State of Israel."

These two landmark documents – the OSCE Berlin Declaration and the IHRA working definition of anti-Semitism – are important affirmations by international organizations of the serious problem of anti-Semitism in the form of the demonization and delegitimization of Israel. Both papers should be disseminated as widely as possible to educate public officials, educators, journalists, and others about the current manifestations of anti-Semitism.

In Latin America, where approximately half a million Jews live, the growing presence of Iran is a primary concern for the Jewish community. In 1992, Iranian-backed Hezbollah was responsible for the Israeli Embassy bombing in Buenos Aires. Two years later came the bombing of the AMIA Jewish community center. While the search for justice continues in those cases, a tour last fall by Iranian Foreign Minister Mohammad Javad Zarif of six Latin American countries signaled Iran's determination to continue sponsoring terrorism, promoting radical Islamic extremism, and strengthening alliances with anti-American regimes.

Iran has established mosques, schools, and other cultural centers within indigenous populations in Latin America, using these institutions to cultivate diplomatic ties with regional governments. Using embassies and consulates staffed largely by intelligence agents, Iran has pursued illicit trade opportunities and money laundering to fund terror. It has also obtained dual-use material for its ballistic missile and nuclear programs.

More than half the Jewish community of Venezuela has fled, in large part because of the anti-Semitic environment facilitated by President Nicolas Maduro and his predecessor, Hugo Chavez. The two leaders have propagated anti-Israel harangues, Holocaust denial, and attacks by government troops on Jewish institutions. In Bolivia, anti-Israel rhetoric by President Evo Morales, who has referred to Israel as a "terrorist state," has also fostered violent attacks on Jewish targets.

Even in Latin American countries that have bilateral relationships with Israel, the overheated anti-Israel rhetoric that follows episodes of hostility in the Middle East redound to the detriment of local Jewish communities. Following Israel's defensive military operation in Gaza in 2014, for example, five Latin American governments – Ecuador, Brazil, Chile, Peru and El Salvador – recalled their ambassadors to Israel and harshly condemned Israel's actions, while largely ignoring attacks by Hamas on Israeli civilians. What followed was an anti-Semitic backlash in some of those countries, leaving Jews fearing for their safety. In Chile, which has a large Palestinian community, Jewish cemeteries were defaced with graffiti and Jewish individuals were verbally attacked in public spaces. In Brazil, the number of émigrés to Israel more than doubled over the next year.

An annual gathering of non-governmental organizations known as the World Social Forum (WSF), founded in Brazil, has become a major platform for the BDS movement. Iran and the Palestinians have used the WSF as a vehicle for gaining legitimacy in international political opinion. This in turn has fueled anti-Semitism by encouraging radical groups who espouse hatred of Jews in the name of confronting Zionism and imperialism.

In light of the dramatic surge in anti-Semitism in recent years, it is essential to continue the difficult struggle against this distinct and uniquely resilient social illness that gave rise to the Holocaust and that persists, in both new and old variations, today. The role of the United States is indispensable in this fight, as no other country can project the same moral leadership and international influence necessary to shine a spotlight on this pressing human rights problem.

RECOMMENDATIONS

1) B'nai B'rith has urged the Administration to appoint a new Special Envoy for Monitoring and Combating Anti-Semitism at the Department of State. This position, created by the landmark Global Anti-Semitism Awareness Act of 2004, has proven an essential tool in the fight against hatred of Jews. When an official can bring the power and prestige of the U.S. government to bear on this human rights problem, the world will take notice that the United States has made fighting anti-Semitism a priority and will hold other countries accountable for their records.

2) B'nai B'rith has also called for the appointment of a special coordinator on anti-Semitism in the United States, to be housed at the Department of Justice. The alarming spike in domestic anti-Semitism in recent months necessitates increased attention by the U.S. government. Such an official at the Justice Department could coordinate cross-agency efforts to tackle anti-Semitism, working with officials at the Federal Bureau of Investigation and the Department of Homeland Security, for example.

3) Congress should pass the Combating European Anti-Semitism Act of 2017, which would require the State Department to report on the security challenges facing European Jewish communities; describe relevant educational programs and law enforcement efforts; and document attempts by European governments to utilize working definitions of anti-Semitism.

4) Congress should pass the Combating BDS Act of 2017, which would allow state and local governments to penalize entities that engage in boycott, divestment, and sanctions activity targeting Israel.

5) Congress should pass the Anti-Semitism Awareness Act, which the Senate passed in the previous session, while the House did not. The legislation would provide the Department

of Education with important definitional assistance in determining whether federal anti-discrimination laws have been violated in educational programs and activities. This will certainly ease the plight of Jewish students who are currently experiencing anti-Semitic harassment on campus.

6) Congress should support a robust level of U.S. foreign aid. The international affairs budget, which represents a mere one percent of the overall federal budget, represents an important investment in U.S. interests abroad. By fighting terrorism, shoring up fragile economies and democratic political systems, and tackling poverty and disease, foreign aid protects vulnerable minorities around the world. The battle against anti-Semitism is greatly aided by this vital soft power tool.